INTERACADEMIC COLLABORATION
Involving Higher Education Institutions in Tlaxcala and Puebla, Mexico.
PRESENTED IN COLLABORATION
with Université Clermont Auvergne (France)

INTERACADEMIC COLLABORATION
Involving Higher Education Institutions in Tlaxcala and Puebla, Mexico.
PRESENTED IN COLLABORATION
with Université Clermont Auvergne (France)

Case studies of collaborative, multidisciplinary applications.

Jose Victor Galaviz Rodriguez
Alexis Christian Charbonnier Poeter
Roman Daniel Romero Mitre

Library of Congress Control Number:		2019912964
ISBN:	Hardcover	978-1-5065-3001-7
	Softcover	978-1-5065-3003-1
	eBook	978-1-5065-3002-4

Print information available on the last page.

First Edition
Rev. date: 04/09/2019

To order additional copies of this book, please contact:
Palibrio
1663 Liberty Drive
Suite 200
Bloomington, IN 47403
Toll Free from the U.S.A 877.407.5847
Toll Free from Mexico 01.800.288.2243
Toll Free from Spain 900.866.949
From other International locations +1.812.671.9757
Fax: 01.812.355.1576
orders@palibrio.com
802170

CONTENTS

Acknowledgements

Universidad Tecnológica de Tlaxcala, Universidad Tecnológica de Tecamachalco, Universidad Tecnológica de Tehuacán, Instituto Tecnológico Superior de la Sierra Norte de Puebla, Instituto Tecnológico Superior de San Martin Texmelucan, Instituto Tecnológico Superior de la Sierra Negra de Ajalpan, Université Clermont Auvergne (France).

Universidad Tecnológica de Tlaxcala
Process Engineering, UTTLAX-CA-2
Business and Marketing, UTTLAX-CA-6
Information Technology & Process and Service Management

Universidad Tecnológica de Tecamachalco
Industrial Process Optimization UTTEPU-CA-5

Universidad Tecnológica de Tehuacán
Industrial Process UTTEH-CA-7

Instituto Tecnológico Superior de San Martin Texmelucan
Strategic Management, Innovation and Education for Competitive Organizational Development ITESSMT-CA-3
Manufacturing Systems Optimization ITESSMT-CA-5

Instituto Tecnológico Superior de la Sierra Norte de Puebla
Engineering Sciences ITESNP-CA-1

Instituto Tecnológico Superior de la Sierra Negra de Ajalpan
Technology and process automation ITSSNA-CA-1

Institut Universitaire de Technologie de Clermont-Ferrand (France)
Département de la Gestion des Entreprises et des Administrations

Coordinating Authors

JOSÉ VÍCTOR GALAVIZ RODRÍGUEZ
ALEXIS CHRISTIAN CHARBONNIER POETER
ROMAN DANIEL ROMERO MITRE

CHAPTER AUTHORS

Jonny Carmona Reyes

Roberto Avelino Rosas

Yolanda González Díaz

Simón Sánchez Ponce

Noemí González León

Leticia Flores Pulido

Edgar Alfredo Portilla Flores

Lorena Santos Espinosa

Susana Monserrat Báez Pimentel

Ma. Luisa Espinosa Águila

Julissa Tizapantzi Sánchez

Adriana Montiel García

José Luis Méndez Hernández

Clara Romero Cruz

Roberto Vega Rocha

Laura Gutiérrez López

Esmeralda Aguilar Pérez

Katia Lorena Avilés Coyoli

Sergio Hernández Corona

Romualdo Martínez Carmona

Sonia López Rodríguez

Margarita Lima Esteban

José Arcángel Zamora García

Eloina Herrera Rodríguez

CHAPTER I

Designs and Molds for Testing New Paint Pigments – A Case Study

**Jonny Carmona Reyes, Roberto Avelino Rosas,
Yolanda González Díaz, Simón Sánchez Ponce**

Abstract A strategic model is used in Mexico in order to create business projects in collaboration with universities. This model is called the Innovation Incentive Program. It finances a percentage of the total cost of a project through which a company plans to innovate a production process or product. The requirement is to collaborate with at least one university. One part of this project was the design and manufacturing of a plastic injection mold which is needed to test new paint pigments in a company. The collaboration began by researching the fundamentals of the plastic mold injection and manufacturing process, which were then implemented into mold design and manufacturing. The project ended in success and the company was pleased with its collaboration with the university.

Keywords Molds, Manufacturing, Design.

1.1 INTRODUCTION

Design and mold making are very important industrial activities to produce goods, so working on a project that involves such areas is a good opportunity to apply knowledge and acquire new skills for participants.

Developing the project involved several phases. The first phase was research on plastic injection molds and the principles of these types of tools. An initial concept was established, because before a mold can be made, a mental image must be produced.

Once the mental image has been formed, it is brought to life by drawing it on paper in the form of a rough sketch. This rough sketch is transformed into a working drawing with dimensions. The working drawing is used to create the shape of the mold (Gingery, 2015).

In the second step, shape designs were drawn using CAD/CAM software for the plastic part to be injected for testing new paint pigments. The best adapted design was selected by the company, and work began.

Once the shape of the plastic part had been selected, research began on the mold design.

1.2 THE PLASTIC INJECTION MOLD

The mold is the most important part of Injection Machine Molding. It is a controllable, complex and expensive device. If not properly designed, operated, handled and maintained, its operation will be costly and inefficient (Rosato, 2000).

Under pressure, hot, melted plastic moves rapidly through the mold. During injection into the mold, air in the cavity or cavities is released to prevent melt burning and the formation of voids in the product. Thermoplastic temperature-controlled water (with ethylene-glycol if water must remain mobile below the freezing point) circulates in the mold to remove heat. With thermosets, electrical heaters are usually used within the mold to provide the additional heat required to solidify the melted plastic in the cavity.

The mold consists of a sprue, a runner, a cavity gate and a cavity. The sprue is the channel located in the stationary plate that transports the melt from the plasticator nozzle to the runner. In turn, melt flows through the runner and enters the cavity. In a single cavity mold, usually no runner is used, so melt goes from the sprue to the gate.

Molds are provided with different means, such as sliders, unscrewing devices, undercuts and knockout systems, to eject products as well as solidified runners at the right time. These basic operations, in turn, require control of various parameters, such as fill time and hold pressure.

To simplify molding, whenever possible, one should design the product with features that simplify the mold-cavity melt filling operation. Many features can improve the product's performance and/or reduce cost. One example is choosing the mold-cavity draft angle according to the plastic being processed and tolerance requirements.

The industry has standardized many of the required elements for building molds. This standardization allows mold makers to order many of the components of the mold by catalog. This allows mold makers to pay more attention to the manufacturing of critical elements such as the cavity and the core blocks (Sapene, 2006).

Therefore, this project focused on working on the design and manufacturing of the cavity and core.

Through our research, we found that injection molds are assemblies of parts in which two blocks, the core and cavity blocks, form an impression or molding. The mold core forms the interior of the molded parts (molding) and the mold cavity forms the exterior faces of the molding. Among all the components, the core and the cavity are the main working parts. The molding is formed in the impression between the core and the cavity and is ejected after the core and cavity are opened. The pair of opposite directions along which the core and cavity are opened are called the parting line (Fu, 2004).

Parting line. The most favorable filling positions are at the parting line and at the low point of the part. Since the expanding reaction mixture displaces the air from the cavity, the displaced air must have an escape outlet at the highest point of the mold, which means that the parting lines pass through the same point, and venting outlets need to be provided at this point. The parting line position determines the location of the mix head, sprue, runner, gate, venting, and removal of the part with all the auxiliary adjuncts that polymerize and are attached to the molding (Dym, 2001).

The injection molding process requires close control over a variety of parameters in order to achieve high quality products at the most effective cost. One of the consequences of this is the need for precise alignment of the mold components to each other and of the mold to the molding machine. Without proper alignment, the mold halves might not line up properly and may cause deviations in wall thickness and improper (and inconsistent) dimensions of the molded part.

Alignment of mold halves. Commonly, the main method of aligning the two mold halves (A and B) is to use leader pins and bushings. There are a variety of designs to incorporate the concept, but the most common is the standard shouldered pin (with or without oil grooves) and a standard corresponding bushing. The shoulder design allows for a single boring to machine holes in both mold halves for precise location of the pin and bushing (Bryce, 1998).

This method of alignment was chosen for the requested mold.

Mold venting. When molds close, air is trapped between the core and cavity walls. This air must be vented in order to completely inflate the container against the mold walls. Venting is accomplished in two ways (Mucio, 1994):

- Most trapped air escapes along the parting line of the two mold halves that have been machined to allow air passage. In many cases, porous inserts are added along the parting line to assist the venting process.
- Vents are machined or drilled into the mold body. The most common position for one of these vents is at the furthest point

4

away from the center of the container, which usually is on a shoulder. A small plug of porous material is also used in this location. The air escapes through the pores in the plugs, through small holes drilled into the back of the mold to meet these plugs and through a clearance slot running from the top of these mold backs. Vents from the next insert and from the tail block of the mold can also be tied into this vent channel.

Insufficient venting can result in weak spots in the container. In severe cases, it

can result in rough container surfaces or even distorted containers, because air trapped between the plastic and the mold does not allow proper contact between the plastic and the mold wall, resulting in insufficient cooling of the container.

There was no need to develop an ejection system because it was agreed to be done manually.

1.3 MACHINING PROCESS

Another reference point for this project was the machining fundamentals that support the manufacturing part.

These fundamentals are detailed as follows.

Machining is the gradual removal of unwanted materials from the workpiece to obtain a finished product of the desired size, shape, and surface quality. This includes metal cutting using single point and multi-point tools, as well as grinding using abrasive wheels (Singal, 2008).

In general, two types of relative motion must be provided for the machining process. The primary motion or cutting motion is the main motion provided by the machine tool to cause relative motion between the tool and workpiece so that the face of the tool approaches the workpiece material. Primary motion accounts for the majority of power requirements for machining operation.

Feed motion is the motion to be provided to the tool or workpiece. When added to the primary motion, it helps the repeated or continuous chip removal to create a machined surface with the desired geometry. The motion may be continuous or in stages. The feed motion absorbs a small portion of the total power required.

Machining is characterized by its versatility and capability of achieving the highest accuracy and surface quality in the most cost-effective manner.

Machining covers a wide range of aspects that should be studied for the proper understanding and selection of a given process. The main objective is to utilize the selected process to machine the component economically at a high rate of production. The part should be machined at levels of accuracy, surface texture, and surface integrity that satisfy the product designer, avoid the need for post-machining and maintain acceptable machining costs. Selecting a machining process is related to many factors such as part features, part material, dimensional and geometric features, surface texture and surface integrity, among others (El-Hofy H., 2018).

On the other hand, the selection of an appropriate machining process depends on a number of factors which include the material, size, weight and complexity of the geometry, labor, equipment and tooling costs, tolerance and surface finish required, strength, quantity and production rate required and overall quality requirements (Scallan, 2003).

The selection of a machining process depends on the dimensional and geometric features of the product. Dimensional tolerance is defined as the permissible or acceptable variation in the dimensions of a part that affect both product design and the machining process selection. The specified tolerance also should be within the range obtained by the selected machining process so as to avoid further finishing operations and increases in production cost.

The shape of a part depends on its function. Since not all machining processes are equally suitable to produce a given part, designers often change the part's shape without affecting its main function to make it easier to machine through group machining processes. Depending on the tool and workpiece motions, cylindrical shapes can be produced by turning, while flat surfaces are machined by shaping and milling. Drilling and boring are also used to produce internal holes. Parts produced by cutting may undergo finish machining by surface and cylindrical grinding. Finish-machined surfaces can also be honed, lapped or super-finished.

Complex shapes require more machine tool motions and complex control systems in several axes, as is the case for CNC machines.

Machining is the removal of unwanted materials from the workpiece so as to obtain a finished product of the desired size, shape, and surface quality. Machining is characterized by its versatility and capability of achieving the highest accuracy and surface quality in the most economical way (El-Hofy, 2014).

The workpiece material specified for the part influences the selection of the machining process. Most materials can be machined by a range of processes, some with a very limited range. The choice of the machining process depends on the desired shape and size, dimensional tolerances, surface finish and quantity required. It also depends not only on technical suitability but also on economic and environmental considerations.

In conventional machining, cutting forces and power depend on the part material's machinability rating. A material that achieves acceptable surface finish, dimensional accuracy and quality of geometrical features has a high machinability rating. On the other hand, materials with high specific energy levels and those causing excessive tool wear have low machinability indexes.

In this case, the material used is aluminum, which can be shaped by milling, so basic milling concepts are next.

In milling processes, material is removed from the workpiece by a rotating cutter. The two basic milling operations are peripheral (plain) milling and face milling. Peripheral milling generates a surface parallel to the axis of rotation, while face milling generates a surface equal to the axis of rotation. Face milling is used for relatively wide flat surfaces (usually wider than 75 mm). End milling, a type of peripheral operation, is generally used for profiling and slotting operations but may be also be used for face milling in pocketing applications (Stephenson, 2016).

Milling processes can be further divided into up (conventional) and down (climbing) milling operations. If the axis of the cutter does not intersect the workpiece, the motion of the cutter due to rotation opposes the feed motion in up (conventional) milling but is in the same direction as the feed motion in down-milling. When the axis of the cutter intersects the workpiece, both up-and down-milling occur at different stages of the rotation. Up-milling is usually preferable to down-milling when the spindle and feed drive exhibit backlash and when the part has large variation in height or a hardened outer layer due to sand casting or flame cutting. In down-milling, there is a tendency for the chip to become wedged between the insert and cutter, causing tool breakage. However, if the spindle and drive are rigid, cutting forces in peripheral down-milling tend to hold the part down on the machine and reduce cutting vibrations.

Milling is a material removal process used widely for machining metal components made of steel, aluminum alloy and titanium alloy in manufacturing industries (Zhang, 2016).

The milling process is distinguished by a rotating tool with one or more teeth that removes material while travelling along various axes with respect to the workpiece (Cheng, 2009).

Milling is a machining process for producing flat, contoured and helical surfaces by means of multiple cutting-edged rotating tools called milling cutters. The workpiece is clamped on the table and given a linear feed against the rotating cutter. The speed of the cutting tool and the rate at which the workpiece travels depends on the kind of material being machined and the material of the cutter (Nagendra, 2003).

In order to define correct parameters in the milling process, it is necessary to take into account the fact that most machining operations are conducted on machine tools with a rotating spindle. Cutting speeds are usually given in feet or meters per minute and these speeds must be converted to spindle speeds in revolutions per minute in order to operate the machine. Conversion is done by use of formulas 1.1 and 1.2 (Ahola, 2014).

For U.S. units:

$$N = 12V/\pi D \qquad (1.1)$$

For metric units:

$$N = 1000V/\pi D \qquad (1.2)$$

Where N is the spindle speed in revolutions per minute (rpm); V is the cutting speed in feet per minute (fpm) for U.S. units and meters per minute (m/min) for metric units. In milling, drilling, reaming and other operations that use a rotating tool, D is the cutter diameter in inches for U.S. units and millimeters for metric units.

Another important formula for the milling process is Eq. 1.3 of feed speed of worktable (Vf) (Ahola, 2014), that is:

$$Vf = fz * z*N \ (mm/min) \qquad (1.3)$$

Where
fz = Feed/tooth
z = Number of teeth
N = Rotation speed of the spindle

The turning process is also necessary in order to manufacture the pin guides of the mold, in other words, the removal of excess material from the workpiece to produce an axisymmetric surface, in which the workpiece (job) rotates in a spindle and the tool moves in a plane perpendicular to the surface velocity of the job at the job-tool contact point. Turning operations are performed on a machine tool called a lathe. In straight turning, the tool moves parallel to the job axis to machine the rotating job in order to produce a cylindrical surface. In taper turning, a conical surface is produced. Form turning is used to produce axisymmetric surfaces of various types. It may be accomplished by using a form tool, using a tracing template or providing simultaneous motion to the tool along longitudinal and radial directions (Prakash M. Dixit, 2008).

The pin guides require taper turning to make the chamber that facilitates assembly operation between the cavity and core of the mold and groove turning to produce the groove to oil the piece.

1.4 CAD/CAM PRINCIPLES

Another fundamental element of this project is the use of CAD/ CAM software to facilitate design and manufacturing. According to Rao (CAD/CAM Principles and Applications, 3rd Edition, 2010), design is an activity that needs to be well organized, and it should take into account all the influences that are likely to be responsible for the success of the product under development. A product can range from a single component which is functional in itself, like a wrench, to the assembly of a large number of components, all of which contribute to the functioning of the part, such an automobile engine.

Computer Aided Design involves any type of design activity which makes use of computers to develop, analyze or modify engineering design (Lalit, 2008)

As Wang (2012) mentions, many of the turnkey CAD/CAM Systems have been enhanced to include advanced features such as finite element modules (FEM) for analysis, numerical control (NC), milling models for generating cutter location (CL), data and solid modelers.

The design process is an iterative procedure, as a preliminary design is made based on the available information and is improved upon as further information is generated (K. Lalit Narayan, 2008).

The design phase begins by drawing the geometry of the product to be manufactured. A drawing is created by an assembly of points, lines, arcs and circles. In computer graphics, drawings are created in a similar manner. Each one of these is called an entity. The drawing entities a user may find in a typical CAD package include (P. Radhakrishnan, 2004): point, line, construction line, multiline, polyline, circle, spline, arc, ellipse, polygon and rectangle.

Geometric models can be broadly categorized into two types:

1. Two-dimensional
2. Three-dimensional

Two-dimensional models were the first to be developed in light of their relatively lesser complexity. However, their utility is limited because of their inherent difficulty in representing complex objects. Their utility lies in many of the low-end drafting packages, or in representing essentially two-dimensional manufacturing applications such a simple turning jobs (axisymmetric), sheet metal punching, flame or laser cutting. Serious CAM applications would be extremely difficult to operate if they started with two-dimensional geometric modeling. Hence, hardly any applications exist with only two-dimensional geometric modelling.

In contrast, three-dimensional geometric modeling can provide all the information required for manufacturing applications. There are a number of ways in which three-dimensional representation can be achieved. The three principal classifications are (Rao, 2006).

1. The line model
2. The surface model
3. The solid or volume model

Referencing the geometry of the design model creates a parametric relationship between the design model and the workpiece. When the design model is changed, all associated NC sequences are updated to reflect the change.

Another part of the project is the use of CAM software. CAM may be defined as the use of computer systems to plan, manage and control the operations of a manufacturing plant through either direct or indirect computer interface with the production resources of the plant. The geometric model generated during the CAD process forms the basis for the CAM process. Various activities in CAM may require different types of information from the CAD process. Interface algorithms

11

are used to extract such information from the CAD database. NC programming, along with ordering tools and fixtures, results from process planning (Chennakesava R. Alavala, 2009).

One important aspect of this project is the shape and draft required to demold a

plastic injected piece. As Helmi A. Youssef (2012) mentions, complex shapes require more machine tool motions and complex control systems, as is the case with CNC machines. Computer Aided Design/Computer Aided Manufacturing (CAD/CAM) is currently used to link the design phase to manufacturing in order to facilitate production and assembly with minimum complexity. Determining the part shape in the design stage may exclude the most economical manufacturing processes. Once the optimum process is identified, the part shape is optimized for the particular process.

1.5 CNC CONCEPTS

Basic concepts like cutting-process-parameters-planning are explained in (Rao, Manufacturing Technology: Metal Cutting and Machine Tools, Volume 2, 2013) as follows. For a given tool and operation selected, the appropriate process parameters are to be selected. These are generally taken from the handbooks supplied by the cutting-tool manufacturer or based on shop experience. It is important, in the context of CNC manufacturing, that the feeds and speeds selected should be as high as possible in order to reduce machining time, consistent with the product quality achieved.

The mold to be machined is worked on in a CNC machine. One critical step in the manufacturing process is preparation of the workpiece, since positioning in NC programming is based on Cartesian coordinates. Therefore, the machinist must establish the position of the coordinate system before machining the part. In conventional machining, it is common to use an edge finder to locate the edges of the workpiece. The machinist will touch the edges of the part with the edge finder and then zero-out either the dials or the

Digital Readout (DRO). All positions are then referenced from this point, the origin of the coordinate system.

CNC machine tools work in much the same way: the part must be located on the table with an edge finder or indicator before it can be machined. The operator will then press buttons to establish the origin of the coordinate system (better known as work zero).

There are several "zeros" we need to understand to set up a job in a CNC machine. First, each machine has a reference position, also known as machine zero or the machine home position. The second zero is workpiece zero (also called the part zero or work zero). The work zero is the origin of the coordinate system in which our part program is written; it is established by edge finding or indicating the workpiece.

The distance from machine zero to work zero is called work offset. Each axis has an offset value that is stored in the offset registry in the MCU. The MCU keeps track of these values and uses them to move the tool to the proper position for machining (Mattson, 2010).

When using CNC machine tools to manufacture a piece it is necessary to understand the G and M-codes that integrate the programs. According to Liou (2007), G-codes are preparatory functions. Preparatory functions include: x-, y- and z- axis movements, thread cutting, radius compensation, canned cycles, circular interpolations, inch or metric measurement system, dimensional input formats, tool feed rates and tool spindle revolutions. M-codes are the miscellaneous functions. Many M-codes are defined by the CNC machine manufacturer for their machines' unique operating characteristics. M-codes control options like program stop, end of program, spindle rotation direction, tool changes, coolant 1 and 2 on/off, clamp and unclamp, and return to program start.

In CAM software, after defining the geometry and dimensions of the piece, the

tools, parameters and operations to machine it, one has to translate this information into G and M codes using a post-processor. According to Liou (2007) the functions of a post-processor include: (1) conversion of tool position in the part coordinate system to the machine coordinate system; (2) processing of linear interpolation and circular interpolation; (3) generation of correct spindle speed, feed rate, tooling, and various machine operation codes; (4) modifying and generating commands that allow for requirements of the NC machine controller; (5) verifying the correctness of tool or part travel range and tool motion, and (6) setting the output format as required by the NC machine.

Some of the major areas in which CNC users can and should expect improvement are:

- Setup time reduction
- Lead time reduction
- Accuracy and repeatability
- Contouring of complex shapes
- Simplified tooling and work holding
- Consistent cutting time
- General productivity increase

Each area offers potential improvement. Individual users will experience different levels of actual improvement depending on the product manufactured on site, the CNC machine used, the setup methods, the complexity of fixtures, the quality of cutting tools, management philosophy and engineering design, experience level of workers and individual attitudes (Smid, 2003).

In this case, due to the complexity of the mold shape and the accuracy required to produce the mold in order to receive the nozzle and assembly itself, CNC machining is the best choice.

1.6 CUTTING TOOL INFORMATION

Cutting tools play an important role in the machining process, so it is necessary to select them well in order to achieve manufacturing, of the mold in this case. As described, milling cutters may be made from a solid piece of HSS or carbide or from a steel shank with replaceable carbide insert cutting edges. Insert carbide cutters come in a variety of shapes and sizes and consist of a cutter body that is usually made of soft steel and disposable carbide inserts. The cutter body has a series of pockets machined around its periphery. Carbide inserts fit in these pockets and are secured with mounting screws. Since the cutting action is performed by the carbide insert portion of the tool, very high cutting speeds can be used, making the inserted carbide cutter a very efficient cutting tool.

In this case, the tool of interest is the endmill type that at first glance resembles a twist drill bit. Endmills have cutting edges both on their end and on the periphery for milling. Endmills are useful when machining a wide variety of features such as pockets, slots, keyways and steps. Flat, general purpose endmills have a straight outside diameter and a flat face on their ends. Specially designed endmills are also available for performing milling functions such as roughing (removing large amounts of material), creating convex radii, concave radii, T-slots, woodruff keyseats and dovetails.

Endmills are available in standard fractional inch and metric diameters and come in a variety of flute counts and styles. Since the flutes form the cutting edges, the number of flutes is the same as the number of cutting edges. The most common flutes counts are two and four, although others are available for special purposes. Selection of the cutting-tool flute number depends on the material to be cut and the cutting conditions. Since each cutting edge removes a certain volume of material, feed rates and depth cut can usually be increased with a higher flute count. Soft material, such as aluminum, generally allows for higher feed rates and produces larger chips as a result. Larger chips require the additional flute space of a two-flute endmill to prevent the flutes from packing with chips. The increased strength and rigidity of a four-flute tool can be beneficial when machining harder materials such as tool steel and stainless steel. The additional cutting edges of a four-flute tool can also help create better surface finishes.

Another tool of interest for this work is the ballnose endmill, which is an endmill with a half-round sphere ground on its end. The radius of the sphere is proportional to the diameter of the outside diameter. A ballmill may be used to mill a concave radius in a workpiece (Peter Hoffman, 2015).

1.7 CASE STUDY

This section presents the development of the project step by step, from the design stage to the manufacturing of the mold.

The design of the mold was made by taking into account the specifications of the plastic injection machine that the company had to produce its parts. In this case, it was a small manual injection machine. Therefore, the dimensions of the plastic part we measured were defined in this context.

Next, we selected the draft angle in order to demold the plastic part. According to Erik Tempelman (2014), a draft angle of 3 degrees is usually sufficient unless the product is deeply textured, so the draft angle for the mold wall was 3 degrees.

Another important issue in mold design was selecting the material to be machined. Due to the nature of the usage (testing new pigments), aluminum 6061 T6 was chosen, because it is an alloy with properties such as strength and lightness. It has excellent finishing features in the machining process, it resists corrosion and it is easy to machine.

The next consideration was the channel where the nozzle was to be placed. This part was designed based on the diameter of the nozzle.

The injection point was set according to the cavity size and the channel vents were designed according to the direction of the injection. The pockets where the pin and bushing guides were to be placed were also considered in this stage.

All the parts that made up the design mold were drawn in a 2-D sketch on CAD/CAM software that allows for the definition of the type of machine, in this case, milling, the operations for geometry, machining parameters and post-processing, to obtain the NC codes.

Manufacturing of the mold includes the planning of each face of the mold plates, the alignment of each plate in the CNC machine table, the roughing and finishing of the cavity and the milling of the injection point, the channels of venting and sitting nozzles and the pocket operations for the pin and bushing guides.

After the machining stage, we had to polish the cavity in order to produce a smooth surface in the mold, resulting in a flat surface free from residual marks from the milling tool.

1.7.1 MOLD DESIGN

A sketch was drawn in the shape of the mold contour in CAD/CAM software using lines and circles in a 90 x 45 mm rectangle, along with the geometries for the injection point (line), air vent (rectangle), sprue channel (line) and the locations for the pin and bushing guides (circles).

The dimensions of these geometries were defined in collaboration between the company and the university according to product size.

The cavity design was also made, based on the dimensional capacity of the machine where the plastic is to be injected, with a draft of 3 degrees and a cavity depth of 4 mm. This way, the material injected in the cavity will be efficiently demolded and the force of the machine used to inject plastic will fill the cavity properly.

The venting location for the mold was placed in the parting line, as suggested by the company.

The logo design was critical because of its complexity. By using a special feature in the CAD/CAM software it was possible to import the original image and then, using the mirror tool, place it inside out as needed.

Part of the design phase involves the definition of tolerance between assembly parts such as the pin and bushing guides and cavity and flat plates. In order for the pin guides and cavity holes to be assembled, an interference fit is defined. For assembly between the pin and bushing guides, a slack fit is selected to allow the pin guides to slide into the bushing guides with level 9 quality. In both cases, the difference between fits is the position for interference, K, and for slack, H.

1.7.2 CAD/CAM Operations

Based on these dimensions, we proceeded to define the operations, tools and machining parameters in order to obtain the machining simulation and then run the post-processor of the CAD/CAM software in order to obtain the CNC codes.

The first operation defined was roughing by means of a pocket to machine the cavity using a 6 mm diameter four-flute flat endmill made of HSS. The feed rate parameter was calculated using Eq. (3) and the spindle speed with Eq. (2), with a cut speed of 45 m/min and 0.15 mm/tooth feed, as recommended by the tool manufacturer.

After these calculations were made, they were saved by entering them in the CAM software.

The first step, once the design is done in CAD/CAM software, is to define the type of machine to be used, which in this case is milling and default.

In doing this, we defined a toolpath group in the Operations Manager of the CAM software. Then it was necessary to define the first operation, generation of the cavity, so the pocket was the right choice in this case.

Next, we selected the tool and type of machining parameters (feed rate, plunge rate and spindle speed). The tool is selected based on the operation and dimensions of the geometry to be machined. In this case, a 6 mm diameter flat endmill was chosen.

When selecting the tool, immediately one must enter the corresponding squares for feed rate and spindle speed. There is also a parameter for plunge rate, which according to CAD/CAM software is half the feed rate, but this speed is too high and it can damage to the tool, so a value obtained from experience is 20 mm/min. It has the disadvantage of taking more time to plunge into the material, but it helps extend the tool's lifetime.

Further information and parameters to consider are the cutting method and stepover percentage. Selection of the cutting method is based on the shape of the part to be machined and the stepover percentage can be manipulated in order to achieve the pocket, because in some cases, from personal experience, not all of the shape is removed due to incorrect stepover percentage. When this happens, one needs to analyze the stepover percentage and adjust this value upwards or downwards. CAM software suggests 75% for the stepover, so this value can be used at first. If in simulation mode one realizes there are leftovers in the pocket, then one must change the value. In the event that CAM automatic calculation is not able to eliminate the leftover, another strategy must be used, such as drawing a line in the pocket and setting up a contour operation to eliminate the material.

Once the cutting method and stepover have been specified, one needs to define cut depth. In this case, it was 0.3 millimeters in the roughing operation with a finish cut of 0.1 millimeters. One must also activate the tapered walls option in order to define the draft (3°) to demold the plastic piece to be injected. The cut depth order must also be defined.

These values are very important to obtain a satisfactory machining time and a well-finished surface. If the cut depth is larger, machining time will decrease but the finished surface may be rougher than expected. On the other hand, a lesser value will increase machining time and surface quality can be almost the same as with the defined cut depths for roughing and finishing.

Next, one must define the default settings for the reference tool, such as clearance, retract, feed plane, top of stock and total depth to cut.

These distances are explained as follows. Clearance is the distance between the tool and the top of the piece as the first and last z-coordinate of the NC program and can be defined in an absolute or incremental reference. In this case it was absolute. Retract is the distance that separates the tool from the workpiece each time the tool finishes an operation and moves to another coordinate to begin another cut. It can also be defined absolutely or incrementally. Feed plane is the distance where the tool starts moving with a programmed speed (plunge rate), absolutely or incrementally. These two last distances should be set incrementally, because in this case machining time is shortened compared to the absolute setting. Top of stock distance is the z-coordinate that defines the z-coordinate zero, and it is necessary to stay in absolute position and at zero value because it is the reference for the workpiece surface. Depth is the total distance that will be machined, either in one or several cuts.

This is the procedure to define the roughing step of the mold cavity. For the finishing stage, we used a 2 mm diameter two-flute ballnose endmill made of carbide. The procedure is similar to the roughing step, while changing operation from pocket to contour and changing the values of the feed rate (300 mm/min), spindle speed (4700), cut depth (0.1 mm) and total depth, in this case 4 mm.

Now it is possible to run the cavity roughing machining simulation and the finishing simulation, as shown in Fig. 1.

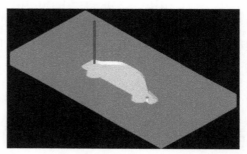

Fig. 1 Cavity finishing machining simulation

Using a similar procedure, we created the toolpath for the plastic injection point through a contour operation with a 2 mm diameter two-flute ballnose endmill made from carbide.

Another important operation was machining of the 0.1 mm depth vent to eject the air trapped in the cavity using a 3/8 in. diameter four-flute endmill.

In order to place the plastic injection machine nozzle in the mold, we had to machine a half-round channel with a ½ in. diameter four-flute ballnose endmill.

Following the operation simulation, the company logo was engraved using a handcrafted tool with a conical tip of 0.5 mm diameter.

CAM software was used one final time to draw and simulate the machining of the holes that served to place the guide pins and bushings that allow for assembly of both halves of the mold.

Once the machining simulations were completed and approved, we proceeded to generate and edit NC programs to machine the mold plates.

Programs generated by CAM software must be edited because some information is not recognized by the CNC machine, such as the number of tools. The CNC machine used to machine the mold recognizes up to 20 tools and CAM software has over 200 tools, so information like this must be corrected.

Another change in the edition mode was matching the T and H variables that stand for the tool and its height. When changing the tool number, height must also be changed. One also needs to eliminate the M01 and A0 codes: the former stops the machine before a tool change and the latter searches for the origin of the fourth axe, which the machine we used does not have. Therefore, when it reaches the line where the code is, an alarm sounds and the machine must be reset.

1.7.3 Mold manufacturing in a CNC Vertical Machining Center

Manufacturing the mold began by aligning the press that holds the workpiece using a dial. This step is critical because if the press is not parallel to the axis of the machine, the mold plates are skewed and they do not assemble correctly. Once alignment has been done, a mold plate is placed in the press and leveled using a water drop level. Once the plate has been leveled, it is fixed to the press.

The first operation to be performed is designing the plate sides using a 12 mm diameter flat endmill by means of an NC program made in the CNC vertical machining center. Following this operation, both plates of the mold were ready to be machined using the mold geometry.

The next operation was roughing the cavity. Preparation of the plate consisted of:

1. Defining the workpiece origin: in this case, it is the center of the plate.

Using a sensor device, it approaches an edge of the plate, first on the x-axis with a grade of 1 mm, then when the device is very close (2 or 3 millimeters) from the endplate, the grade changes to 0.1 mm and it continues moving until it touches the plate, then it retracts 0.1 mm and changes to 0.01 mm and it repeats this approach until it touches the plate, then it retracts and changes the grade to 0.001 mm, which is the lowest grade of the machine, and it touches the plate surface. Touching occurs when a red light flashes on the device. Next, a value of the x-axis may be observed on the CNC machine, and it is recorded. The device is retracted and moved to the other side of the plate on the x-axis and the process is repeated. Once the two x-axis values have been obtained, the difference between both values is calculated and divided in half, indicating the center of the plate.

2. This procedure is repeated in order to find the value center of the y-axis.
3. Both the x and y-axes are moved to the calculated coordinates and these values are recorded in the G54 or G55 to G155 of the CNC. In this case, G54 is the physical origin of the workpiece.
4. The height of each tool to be used in machining operations must be determined. This is done by placing the tool in the spindle and approaching it to the piece in the previously defined center. Approaching is carried out in 1 mm grades. When the tool is close to the workpiece, the grade is changed to 0.1 mm until it touches the plate, then it is retracted to 0.1 mm and it is changed to 0.01 mm and touching is repeated. Finally, the grade is changed to 0.001 mm until it touches the plate. Touching is confirmed by placing a sheet of aluminum foil between the tool and the plate so that when the tool approaches the plate it moves the aluminum foil and continues approaching until the tool grasps the aluminum foil. The thickness of the aluminum foil is added in order to obtain the value of the tool height, which is then stored in the CNC vertical machining center.

The CNC program must be immediately loaded on the CNC board of the vertical machining center using a USB device. Once the program has been loaded, it must be checked in graphic mode in order to check that there are no mistakes in the edition of the program. If there are any mistakes, a red light flashes on the board and a warning message is displayed. The board must then be reset and the mistake corrected. If there are no mistakes, simulation of machining ends and the code M30 appears on the display.

This process must be followed in each CNC program to be run if the original workpiece and tools are different.

For the cavity plate, we just changed the height of the tools. In this case, five endmills were used, a 6 mm diameter flat endmill to machine the cavity roughing and the holes for the pin guides, a 2 mm diameter ballnose endmill to machine the cavity finishing and the injection point, a ½ inch diameter ballnose endmill was used to machine the sprue, a 12 mm diameter flat endmill was used to machine the air vent and a handicraft point endmill was used to engrave the company logo.

For the other flat plate, we used three endmills: a ½ inch diameter ballnose endmill to machine the sprue, a 2 mm diameter ballnose endmill to machine the other half of the injection point and a 6 mm diameter flat endmill to machine the holes for the bushing guides.

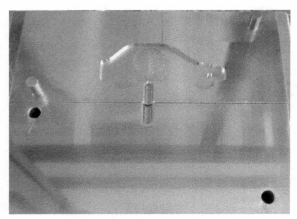

Fig. 2. Finished mold plates

1.7.4 Polishing mold plates

We had to polish the plates because when they left the CNC vertical machining center there were lots of tool marks on them. To polish them, we used sandpaper beginning with grade 320 manually to remove the largest marks, changing to 600, 1200 and finally 1500 grade sandpaper. Then, we applied polishing paste with a rag in order to obtain a mirror appearance. The results can observed in Fig. 2.

1.7.5 Assembly of pin guides

Another important operation was turning the pin guides by chamfering both ends in a lathe machine using a 2 mm x 45° chamfer. This operation facilitates their assembly into the cavity plate.

Assembly of the pin guides was performed using a 1-ton press with a K9 fit in order to ensure that assembly in the cavity plate was made with interference. The difference between the hole and pin diameters is 0.043 mm, since the diameter reference is 12.7 mm. According to ISO quality standards, the tolerance in a range from 10 to 18 mm is 43 microns. Results were satisfactory.

1.8 RESULTS

The plastic injection mold was tested by injecting plastic with the new pigments in it. The pieces obtained were those expected by the company. Table 1 shows the machining and polishing times required to manufacture this mold.

Table 1. Operation times

Item	Operation	Time (min)
1	Cavity roughing	105.25
2	Cavity finishing	74.1
3	Logo engraving	5.5

4	Sprue machining (cavity)	15.3
5	Injection point (cavity)	2.5
6	Vent machining	4.3
7	Pin guide holes	3.4
8	Sprue machining (flat plate)	15.3
9	Injection point (flat plate)	2.5
10	Bushing guides	3.5
11	Polishing of cavity plate	95
12	Polishing of flat plate	61.5
	Total	388.15

Manufacturing time was satisfactory because the proper tools were used and the machining parameters were properly calculated based on equations.

With regards to the functionality of the mold, it took two weeks to be completed once the design had been finalized. The process followed was: company requirements, principles of plastic injection mold systems, CAD/CAM software operations, knowledge of milling operations and tools and the application of manufacturing operation skills in the use of a vertical machining center. The workpieces were well prepared, so theory and practice together led to great results.

1.9 CONCLUSIONS

When universities and companies work together they can obtain good results, as occurred in this case. The experience of company personnel was complemented by academic knowledge based on methodologies that have proved to be successful, such as using data, equations, principles and experience in the application of theory in practical cases.

The reciprocal communication between the company and the university was a critical activity that worked well. It accelerated the design and decision-making processes, allowing participants to define and resolve several issues. Positive results were achieved because of the willingness of both entities to succeed.

The investigation of new CAD/CAM features facilitated design and operations planning, which in this case was the option of importing a complicated shape, the company logo.

Analysis of the entire project and its corresponding results in order to develop it step by step was very important in achieving the transition from the idea to producing the physical mold in a relatively short time.

The opportunity to work on projects like this develops the skills of the people involved. The Mexican model of working with companies and universities can lead to great developments in the technological field. It's a win-win way of working.

Last but not least, materials procurement is very important. If there are no raw materials or tools, it is impossible to work and transform plain plates into useful tools. In this case, all the tools and materials were available when needed.

1.10 REFERENCES

Ahola, J. (2014). *Creo Parametric Milling.* Klaava Media.

Bryce, D. M. (1998). *Plastic Injection Molding... mold design and construction fundamentals.* Society of Manufacturing Engineers.

Cheng, K. (2009). *Machining Dynamics, Fundamentals, Applications and Practices.* Springer.

Chennakesava R. Alavala. (2009). *CAD/CAM Concepts and Applications.* PHI Learning Private Limited.

Dym, J. (2001). *Injection Molds and Molding: A Practical Manual.* Kluwer Academic Publishers.

El-Hofy, H. A.-G. (2014). *Fundamentals of Machining Processes Conventional and Nonconventional Processes.* CRC Press Taylor and Francis.

Erik Tempelman, H. S. (2014). *Manufacturing and Design understanding the principles of how things are made*. Oxford, UK: Butterworth-Heinemann.

Fu, J. (2004). *Computer-Aided Injectio Mold Design and Manufacture*. Marcel Dekker Inc.

Gingery, V. R. (2015). *Secrets of Building A Plastic Injection Molding Machine*. David J. Gingery Publishing.

Helmi A. Youssef, H. A.-H. (2012). *MANUFACTURING TECHNOLOGY Materials, Processes and Equipment*. CRC Press Taylor and Francis Group.

K. Lalit Narayan, K. R. (2008). *Computer Aided Design and Manufacturing*. Prentice Hall of India Private Limited.

Liou, F. W. (2007). *RAPID PROTOTYPING AND ENGINEERING APPLICATIONS A Toolbox for Prototype Development*. CRC Press Taylor and Francis Group.

Mattson, M. (2010). *CNC Programming Principles and Applications Second Edition*. DELMAR CENGAGE Learning.

Mucio, E. A. (1994). *Plastic Processing Technology*. ASM International.

Nagendra, B. (2003). *Elements of Manufacturing Processes*. PHI Learning Private Limited New Delhi.

P. Radhakrishnan, S. S. (2004). *CAD/CAM/CIM Second Edition*. New Age International Publishers.

Peter Hoffman, E. H. (2015). *Precision Machining Technology Second Edition*. CENGAGE Learning.

Prakash M. Dixit, U. S. (2008). *Modeling of Metal Forming and Machining Processes by Finite Element and Soft Computing Methods*. Springer-Verlag London Limited.

Rao, P. (2006). *CAD/CAM Principles and Applications Second Edition*. Tata McGraw Hill Education Private Limited.

Rao, P. (2010). *CAD/CAM Principles and Applications 3rd Edition*. Tata McGraw Hill Education Private Limited.

Rao, P. (2013). *Manufacturing Technology: Metal Cutting and Machine Tools Volume 2*. Mc Graw Hill Education (India) Private Limited.

Sapene, C. (2006). *Cost Analysis of Plastic Injection Molds.* Injection Mold Solutions.

Scallan, P. (2003). *Process Planning.* Butterworth-Heinemann.

Smid, P. (2003). *A Comprehensive Guide to Practical Programming CNC Programming Handbook.* New York: Industrial Press Inc.

Wang, P. C. (2012). *Advances in CAD/CAM Case Studies.* Springer Science and Bussiness Media.

Zhang, W. (2016). *Milling Simulation Metal Milling Mechanics, Dynamics and Clamping Principles.* ISTE Ltd.

CHAPTER II

Optimization of Containers for Christmas Tree Ornaments Through Differential Evolution

Noemí González León, Leticia Flores Pulido, Edgar Alfredo Portilla Flores, Lorena Santos Espinosa.

Abstract This article presents a proposed algorithm called NOEA for the optimization of the production of containers for Christmas tree ornaments, with the purpose of modeling the process of a blister and swaging machine in such a way that production meets demand, using necessary resources to perform its tasks and saving energy. For future research, comparative analysis of the convergence of the iL-SHADE, C-LSHADE algorithms and the proposed algorithm is planned. This study is the result of the work carried out by the Information Technology and Information Systems Division of the Higher Technological Institute of the Sierra Norte de Puebla, the National Polytechnic Institute, CIDETEC, in Mexico City, and the School of Basic Sciences and Engineering of the Autonomous University of Tlaxcala, Mexico.

Keywords Optimization, Container, Differential evolution, Blister machine, Swaging

2.1 INTRODUCTION

Over the past 40 years, the town of Chignahuapan, Puebla has become famous for producing hand blown glass Christmas tree ornaments. Over 350 workshops and six factories are dedicated to the producing ornaments. According to Luis Ángel Rojas Lecona, a single factory can produce at least 10 million ornaments. In 2012, more than 300 million ornaments were produced. They are exported to the United States, Central and South America, including Argentina, and Italy.

The ornament production process ends in packaging. One of the greatest challenges facing industry in the region is developing ornament packaging for the distribution, transportation, storage, handling and sale of the product so that it can reach the customer in optimal condition. Packaging provides a competitive advantage over competing products of similar quality.

There are different types of packaging. The material used for most ornaments is cardboard. The drawback of this material is that it does not support much weight. This packaging method is frequently used by smaller factories, causing losses of up to three broken ornaments per box. Another packaging material widely used by ornament producers is a combination of polyvinyl chloride, also known as PVC, and cardboard.

In the Sierra Norte de Puebla, a temperate, cold, humid climate prevails for most of the year which is disadvantageous to the use of carton made in the region, since in these environmental conditions the container becomes soft, causing loss of product. The production process for cylindrical PVC ornament containers is currently done manually. For the caps of the container, the PVC material is thermoformed; for assembly of the cylinder body, a square is cut using a paper cutter, a hand cutter or scissors, then glue is used to join the sides of the material. Finally, a cord is placed on the perforated covers of the container to keep the ornament in place.

The best-selling package is 60 ornaments. PVC caliber is 3.5 inches, and approximately 23,000 packages per year of this material are consumed per workshop or small producer. One person can produce 50 cylindrical PVC containers manually per day. Our proposal seeks to improve the quality of the cylindrical packaging manufacturing process to store 60 ornaments using a blister machine and a mixer to generate an optimal solution that guarantees quality packaging.

Until now, it was widely assumed which shape packaging needed to have to store, transport, and keep Christmas ornaments in good condition. A procedure has already been established, through which it is possible to construct appropriate packaging for the online production of such a design. It is therefore possible, by way of intelligent electronic design through Differential Evolution, to define the construction and online production of appropriate packaging for blown glass Christmas tree ornaments. Production of such packaging must meet the standards and appropriate measures for the intelligent technique to achieve the design properly.

Packaging can be classified into three categories: flexible, semi-rigid, and sealants or adhesives. Semi-rigid ones are thicker than 0.127 mm, flexible ones have a thickness of less than 0.127 mm, and sealants or adhesives require multiple layers, typically requiring heat and pressure. Currently, on the U.S. market containers dominate 51 percent of the total market.

2.2 OPTIMIZATION PROBLEM

The single objective numerical optimization problem is described from Fig. 1 to Fig. 7, to obtain a solution to the design problem and minimize resources used in production of packaging for Christmas ornaments (see Fig. 3). This is done through an adequate definition of the representation of an individual, so that valid individuals are always generated. The representation of each of the terms of the fitness function can be seen in Fig. 4 and 5.

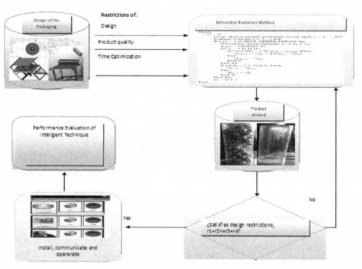

Fig. 3. Process for the optimal design of the container

Process for the optimal design of the container:

$$Minf(p) = (-pd + \alpha po - ps - \beta pf) + sc, p \in R^5 \qquad (1)$$

In which:

f: Fitness or fitness function

pd: Waste area

pf: Area outside the penalized rectangle

po: Occupied area

ps: Overlapping area

sc: Cylinder side surface

β: 2000

The vector of design variables for the mechanism is symbolized by:

$$p = [p1, p2, p3, p4, p5]^T \qquad (2)$$

In which g is a generation index

32

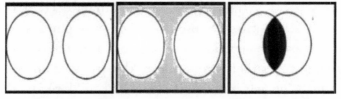

Fig. 4. a). Occupied area b). Waste area c). Overlapping area

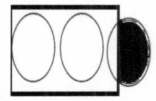

Fig. 5. Area outside the penalized rectangle

The restrictions of the problem during evolution are subject to:

$$po \leq 1000cm^2 \qquad (3)$$

$$pd \leq 14cm^2 \qquad (4)$$

$$ps \leq 0cm^2 \qquad (5)$$

$$pf \leq 0.02cm^2 \qquad (6)$$

$$sc \leq 0.336cm^2 \qquad (7)$$

2.3 METHODOLOGY

Evolutionary stochastic search algorithms are based on Charles Darwin´s principle of survival of the fittest. They consist of the following components:

-Structures that replicate (individuals)
-A fitness function
-A selection mechanism (probabilistic)
-Operators that act on individuals (crosses or mutation)

Evolutionary algorithms are based on a set of randomly generated solutions (populations). For each solution, a value is calculated which usually corresponds to the objective function that we seek to optimize: this value is called fitness. Subsequently, a set of parents is selected to which at least one genetic operator (cross or mutation) is applied, with a certain probability level, that is, the operator does not apply to all parents. The new individuals are called children and they later mutate. These new individuals constitute a new population that will partially or totally replace the previous one.

2.4 RESULTS

The model starts with the parameter vectors P population of the differential evolution algorithm, with NP parameter vectors of D dimensions, where each parameter can be restricted to a range of value as established by restrictions 3 to 7.

Table 2. Population of individuals

Population	Individual 1	Individual 2	Individual 3	Individual 4	Individual 5
P1	1	0.4408137	0.9914455	0.1205224	0.01585685
P2	0.14	0.03533931	0.14298802	038374385	0.21703374
P3	0	0.55045648	0.97302934	0.66750811	0.285156
P4	0.02	0.86189587	0.93442697	0.94863115	0.17140761
P5	0.336	0.93173978	0.00991035	0.77892231	1.22168809
F(p)	1.496	2.82024514	3.05180018	2.89932782	0.9111423

Through differential mutation, we add the proportional difference of two individuals, V2 and V3, chosen randomly from the stable population (V1, individual, target), also chosen randomly. The new individual M_i is called a mutated individual or mutated vector.

$$M_i = V1 + \mu \ (V2 - V3) \qquad (8)$$

Table 3 shows the calculation of the vector of weighted difference between individuals 2 and 5 as well as the proportional difference, which results from multiplying μ by 0.80.

Table 3. Calculation of the weighted difference vector

Population	Individual 2	Individual 2	Difference		Proportional difference
P1	0.4408137	0.01585685	0.42495685		0.339965483
P2	0.03533931	0.21703374	-0.18169444		-0.145355549
P3	0.55045648	0.285156	0.26530048	μ=0.80	0.21224038
P4	0.86189587	0.17140761	0.69048826		0.552390605
P5	0.93173978	1.22168809	0.71005169		0.568041352
F(p)	2.82024514	0.9111423	1.90910284		1.527282272

The mutation constant $\mu > 0$ establishes the range of differentiation between individuals V2 and V3 with the aim of avoiding stagnation in the search process. After mutation, a recombination operation was performed on each individual V1 (target) in order to generate an individual or test vector F_i. Test individual F is controlled by the condition function established in (9):

$$F_i(j) = \begin{cases} M_i(j), \text{if rand} \leq \text{CR} \\ V_i(j) \end{cases} \qquad (9)$$

The selection operator decides on the basis of best fitness. If test individual F_i is accepted and replaces the test individual, F_i is rejected and the target individual is retained in the next generation.

M_i, the mutated vector, and the target vector Vi select a number between 0 and 1. If the condition in Formula 9 is not fulfilled, the first position moves to the second position and moves to the first position of the test vector. Table 2 shows the population of individuals that comprise it.

Table 4 shows the calculation performed to obtain the mutated vector.

Table 4. Obtaining the mutated vector

Population	Proportional difference		Individual 4	Mutated Vector M_i
P1	0.339965483		0.1205224	0.46048788
P2	-0.145355549		038374385	0.2383883
P3	0.21224038	+	0.66750811	0.87974849
P4	0.552390605		0.94863115	1.50102175

P5	0.568041352	0.77892231	1.34696367
F(p)	1.527282272	2.89932782	4.42661009

The index gives the position of each individual, operates to generate values to check against CR, and depending on the condition, transfers the value to the test vector. Next, a random number is selected between 0 and 1 and assigned to CR. A random number is obtained and compared with CR. If it is lower, the value of the mutated vector is passed on, as long as the condition in equation 9 is satisfied

Table 5. Calculation of the test vector

Population	Vector Target (V_j)		Mutated Vector (M_j)	Vector Test (F_j)
P1	1		0.46048788	1
P2	0.14		0.2383883	0.14
P3	0	CR= 0.3349	0.87974849	0
P4	0.02		1.50102175	0.02
P5	0.336		1.34696367	0.336
F(p)	1.496		4.42661009	1.496

When comparing the result of the test vector with the objective vector, we noticed that there is no change in the test vector, so the target vector continues when the crossing factor is Cr = 0.3349. However, when Cr = 1, the test vector is calculated and the first generation is obtained, since the result of the test vector is smaller than the target vector, as seen in Table 5. This gave rise to the first generation of the present study.

Table 6. Calculation of the test vector for the First Generation when F=1.05487618 Cr= 1.

Population	Vector Target (V_j)		Mutated Vector (M_j)	Vector Test (F_j)
P1	1		0.46048788	0.46048788
P2	0.14		0.2383883	0.2383883
P3	0	CR= 1	0.87974849	0

P4	0.02	1.50102175	0.02
P5	0.336	1.34696367	0.336
F(p)	1.496	4.42661009	1.05487618

Design of the upper and lower lid of the container or blister pack was done in SolidWorks 2015 for the subsequent production of the aluminum mold for thermoforming of the PVC material.

Table 7. NOEA Algorithm

Algorithm 1 NOEA

Require: entries are written for the target vector.

Ensure: existing values are displayed.

1:   Start

2:   VectorObjective, V2, V3, V4, difference, proportional difference, VM and VP are declared

3:   **VectorObjective [1]= 1;**

4:   **VectorObjective [2]= 0.14;**

5:   **VectorObjective [3]= 0;**

6:   **VectorObjective [4]= 0.02;**

7:   **VectorObjective [5]= 0.336;**

8:   **CR= 1;**

9:   **to write VectorObjective**

10:   **for** x=1 to 5 **do**

11:   *VectorObjective(x);*

12:   *sum=sum+VectorObjective(x);*

13:   **end for**

14:   **Write "Sum of Objective Vector:", sum**

15:   **Write "Vector Values V2"**

16:   **for** x=1 to 5 **do**

17:   *V2(x)=rand();*

18:   *Write V2(x);*

19:   **end for**

20:   **Write "Vector Values V3"**

21:   **for** x=1 to 5 **do**

22:   *V3(x)=rand();*

23: *Write V3(x);*

24: **end for**

25: **Write "Vector Values V4"**

26: **for** x=1 to 5 **do**

27: *V4(x)=rand();*

28: *Write V4(x);*

29: **end for**

30: **Write "The Vector Difference data are:"**

31: **for** x=1 to 5 **do**

32: *difference(x)=V2(x)-V3;*

33: *Write difference(x);*

34: **end for**

35: **Write "Values of the proportional difference:"**

Table 8. NOEA Algorithm (continued)

36: **for** x=1 to 5 **do**

37: *ProportionalDifference(x)=difference(x)*0.80;*

38: *Write difference(x);*

39: **end for**

40: **Write "Values of the Muted Vector:"**

41: **for** x=1 to 5 **do**

42: *VM(x)=ProportionalDifference(x)+V4(x);*

43: *Write VM(x);*

44: **end for**

45: **NCR=rand();**

46: **Write NCR;**

47: **if NCR<CR then**

48: *VP(1)=VM(1);*

49: **Or**

50: *VP(1)=VectorObjective(1);*

51: **end if**

52: **NCR=rand();**

53: **Write NCR;**

54: **if NCR<CR then**

55: *VP(2)=VM(2);*

56: **Or**

57: *VP(2)=VectorObjective(2);*

58: **end if**

59: **NCR=rand();**

60: **Write NCR;**

61: **if NCR<CR then**

62: *VP(3)=VM(3);*

63: **Or**

64: *VP(3)=VectorObjective(3);*

65: **end if**

66: **NCR=rand();**

67: **Write NCR;**

68: **if NCR<CR then**

69: *VP(4)=VM(4);*

70: **Or**

71: *VP(4)=VectorObjective(4);*

72: **end if**

73: **NCR=rand();**

Table 9. NOEA Algorithm (continued)

74: **Write NCR;**

75: **if NCR<CR then**

76: *VP(5)=VM(5);*

77: **Or**

78: *VP(5)=VectorObjective(5);*

79: **end if**

80: *VP(1)=VectorObjective(1);*

81: **end if**

82: **for** x=1 to 5 **do**

83: *sumVP=sumVP+VP(x);*

84: **end for**

85: Write "Algorithm result"

86: **if sumVP<sum then**

87: *Write "The new generation is given by the test vector VP";*

88: **for** x=1 to 5 **do**

89: *Escribir VP(x);*

90: **end for**

91: **Write "Sum of the test vector is:", sumVP;**

92: *Or*

93: *"the values of the target vector of the previous generation are left:";*

94: *Write VectorObjetive(x);*

95: **end if**

In order to develop the NOEA algorithm, overleaf software was used. In Table 6, 7 and 8 the algorithm used is shown. It was programmed in Octave, as can be seen in Fig. 6.

```
1    disp("Evolución Diferencial NOEA");
2    VectorObjetivo=[1;0.14;0;0.02;0.336]
3    V2=rand(5,1)
4    V3=rand(5,1)
5    Diferencia1= V2-V3
6    DiferenciaProporcional= Diferencial * 0.80
7    V4=rand(5,1)
8    VectorMutado= DiferenciaProporcional + V4
9    CR= 1
10   NCR=rand
11   if NCR < CR
12       disp( "Se saca un número aleatorio y se compara si es menor con el factor
                de cruza, si es menor")
13       disp( "toma el valor del vector mutado para formar el primer elemeto del
                Vector de Prueba")
14       VectorMutado(1,1)
15       VectorPrueba(1,1)=VectorMutado(1,1)
16   else
17       disp( "toma el valor del vector objetivo")
18       VectorObjetivo(1,1)
19       VectorPrueba(1,1)=VectorObjetivo(1,1)
20   end
21   NCR1=rand
22   if NCR1 < CR
23       disp( "Se saca un número aleatorio y se compara si es menor con el factor
                de cruza, si es menor")
24       disp( "toma el valor del vector mutado para formar el primer elemeto del
                Vector de Prueba")
25       VectorMutado(2,1)
26       VectorPrueba(2,1)=VectorMutado(2,1)
27   else
28       disp( "toma el valor del vector objetivo")
29       VectorObjetivo(2,1)
30       VectorPrueba(2,1)=VectorObjetivo(2,1)
31   end
32   NCR2=rand
33   if NCR2 < CR
34       disp( "Se saca un número aleatorio y se compara si es menor con el factor
                de cruza, si es menor")
35       disp( "toma el valor del vector mutado para formar el primer elemeto del
                Vector de Prueba")
36       VectorMutado(3,1)
37       VectorPrueba(3,1)=VectorMutado(3,1)
38   else
39       disp( "toma el valor del vector objetivo")
40       VectorObjetivo(3,1)
41       VectorPrueba(3,1)=VectorObjetivo(3,1)
42   end
43   NCR3=rand
44   if NCR3 < CR
45       disp( "Se saca un número aleatorio y se compara si es menor con el factor
                de cruza, si es menor")
46       disp( "toma el valor del vector mutado para formar el primer elemeto del
                Vector de Prueba")
47       VectorMutado(4,1)
48       VectorPrueba(4,1)=VectorMutado(4,1)
49   else
50       disp( "toma el valor del vector objetivo")
51       VectorObjetivo(4,1)
52       VectorPrueba(4,1)=VectorObjetivo(4,1)
53   end
54   NCR4=rand
55   if NCR4 < CR
56       disp( "Se saca un número aleatorio y se compara si es menor con el factor
                de cruza, si es menor")
57       disp( "toma el valor del vector mutado para formar el primer elemeto del
                Vector de Prueba")
58       VectorMutado(5,1)
59       VectorPrueba(5,1)=VectorMutado(5,1)
60   else
61       disp( "toma el valor del vector objetivo")
62       VectorObjetivo(5,1)
63       VectorPrueba(5,1)=VectorObjetivo(5,1)
64   end
65   SumaVP=sum(VectorPrueba)
66   if SumaVP<SumaVO
67       disp( "La nueva generación esta dada por:")
68       VectorPrueba
69   else
70       disp( "Se deja los datos del Vector Objetivo dado por:")
71       VectorObjetivo
72       SumaVO=sum(VectorObjetivo)
73   end
```

Fig. 6. NOEA Algorithm Programming in Octave

We reviewed literature on the topic and focused on Fellows, who in 2009 used the thermoforming method for sealing and filling rigid containers, achieving saving of 10 to 15 percent of product. In 2017, Fellows achieved a reduction in the cost, energy and consumption of materials. One of the drawbacks he found was seals. Since they are the weakest part of a container, they can break during production.

Mohammad, et al. (2015), studied the elastic behavior of the blister and how to improve performance of the material. We also reviewed the packaging modeling by Li (2017) for the characteristics of containers permeable to moisture.

We proposed to solve the optimization problem using restrictions associated with a mechanism from Vega-Alvarado, et al. (2014). They used a modified differential evolution algorithm, applying tournament type selection, based on the feasibility rules of Deb. The algorithm produced an improvement in decision making to conform the next generation and good engineering design results without requiring extensive computing resources, as well as favorable response time.

Zapata et al. (2017), who adapted an L-SHADE algorithm automatically to parameters with mutation (F) and crossing (CR) through parameter memory, controlling population (NP) using a linear function, incorporated restriction management strategy to L-SHADE in order to optimize three case studies of a four-bar mechanism called C-LSHADE, compared their performance with DE/rand/1/bin using random parameters to solve mechanical optimization problems, and performed an experiment on it. They compared the results obtained by the two algorithms and another in which they analyzed convergence behavior. To validate the data obtained, they used the Wilcoxon rank sum test with a level of significance of 95%. C-LSHADE obtained a better result of DE/rand/1/bin. They concluded that C-LSHADE is able to find better or equal solutions than DE. The percentage of evaluations of the objective function is less than DE, freeing the user from adjusting parameters F, CR and NP. The main modification was to add to the feasibility criteria proposed by DEB in the corresponding stage of best individual. The algorithm was able to find better solutions faster, freeing the user from making manual adjustments of parameters based on trial and error.

Finally, we consulted Brest, et al. (2016), who proposed an extended version of L-SHADE called iL-SHADE to solve problems of optimization of real parameters with a single objective. They performed experiments in 30 reference and four-dimensional functions and were more competitive than the original L-SHADE. The iL-SHADE algorithm differed from L-SHADE in the use of the update mechanism, which stored the historical memory values of the previous generation and used them to calculate the values of historical memory for the next generation, memory H entries, one of them containing fixed values. This entry is not updated, but its values are used to generate the CR_i and F_i control parameters, all historical memory values in M_{CR} are initialized to 0.8, and if M_{CR} is assigned the terminal value, M_{CR} is reset to 0.0.

2.5 CONCLUSIONS

When performing verification of the test vector value with CR, Table 5 shows that the sum of the test vector is 1.05487618, which is lesser than the sum of the target vector, giving rise to the first generation when the cross factor is equal to 1. An improvement in the design of the blister lids was achieved in the fifth iteration.

2.6 FUTURE WORK

We would like to conduct an experiment, a study, a comparative analysis of the convergence of the iL-SHADE algorithms and C-LSHADE in their most recent version along with the present proposal, in order to compare their performance.

2.7 REFERENCES

1. García - de Loera, F.: Creation of spheres in Chignahuapan. http://wikipuebla.poblanerias.com/galeria-elaboracion-de-esferas-en-chignahuapan/, (Retrieved on July 31, 2017)
2. Follows: Felling and sealing of containers. Elsevier. 26. pp. 782-803 (2009)

3. Follows: Felling and sealing of containers. Elsevier. 25. pp. 1045-1076 (2017)

4. Mohammad S. I. and Liyong T.: Effects of initial blister radius and shaft diameter on energy release rate of metal-polymer composite coating, International Journal of Adhesion and Adhesives, (2015). pp 1-35. http://dx.doi.org/10.1016/j. ijadhadh.2015.07.007.

5. Li, Y. and Chen, Y.: Modeling in pharmaceutical packaging, AbbVie Inc., North Chicago, IL, United States, No vast Laboratories, Ltd., Nantong, China. 12. pp. 317-341 (2017)

6. Vega-Alvarado, E., Santiago-Valentin, E., Sánchez-Marquez, A., Portilla-Flores E-A., Flores-Pulido, L.: Optimum synthesis of a flat mechanism for trajectory tracking using differential evolution. In Computing Science. pp. 85-98 (2014).

7. Zapata-Zapata, M-F., Mezura-Montes, E., Portilla-Flores E-A.: Differential evolution with parameter memory for the optimization of four-bar mechanisms. In Computing Science. pp. 9-22 (2017)

8. Brest, J., Sepesy, M.M., Boskovi\'c, B.: iL-SHADE: Improved L-SHADE Algorithm for Single Objetive Real-Parameter Optimization. In: IEEE, F., Editor, S. (eds.) CONGRESS ON EVOLUTIONARY COMPUTATION 2016, pp. 1188-1195.Vancouver, BC, Canada. https://doi.org/10.1109/CEC.2016.7743922

9. Brest, J., Sepesy, M.M., Boskovi\'c, B.: iL-SHADE: Improved L-SHADE Algorithm for Single Objetive Real-Parameter Optimization. In: IEEE, F., Editor, S. (eds.) CONGRESS ON EVOLUTIONARY COMPUTATION 2016, pp. 1188-1195. Vancouver, BC, Canada. https://doi.org/10.1109/CEC.2016.7743922

CHAPTER III

Comprehensive Communications Plan - E.J.K. Chemical, S.A. de C.V

Susana Monserrat Báez Pimentel, Ma.
Luisa Espinosa Águila, Julissa Tizapantzi
Sánchez and Adriana Montiel García.

Abstract A comprehensive communications plan means planning all aspects of communications in a coordinated manner, because there is nothing more unproductive than a company that addresses its audiences differently. Would you trust people who changed their personality when it suited them? People with different faces cannot be trusted, right? This Proposal for a Comprehensive Communications Plan for E.J.K. Chemical, S.A. de C.V. constitutes a proposal by which the company can expand its scope in its city, state and country. It is based on the importance of the relationship of the institution with its internal and external audiences. Companies nowadays create communication forums and strategies which allow them to create harmony among their different audiences in order to successfully meet their objectives. The study we performed on the audience of E.J.K. Chemical, S.A. de C.V identified needs, suggestions, observations and criticisms, allowing us to propose successful communication strategies in this plan in order to better resolve internal and external flaws. Based on the observations and comments obtained, we were able to determine that a public relations department is needed for the organization to establish effective communication tools and strategies to reach the company's internal audience and external public through communication processes and strategies.

3.1 INTRODUCTION

Most successful companies at the local, regional or global level recognize the need for organizational communication departments, obtaining positive results and contributing to better development of their companies.

An organization that plans its communications can more easily reach its sales, corporate, institutional and social objectives. Planning messages and contact procedures is as logical as planning financial, technical or human resources. However, this had not been incorporated into the company's management process.

Currently, communications between companies and their customers is changing. It is increasingly common for companies to use digital media in order to establish more direct or emotional links with their market. It is essential to perform an analysis that helps determine the type of media that should be used to efficiently and effectively reach both internal and external customers.

A comprehensive communications plan uses different means to carry out its task appropriately, such as advertising, direct marketing, sales promotion, personal sales, public relations, digital marketing and alternative marketing. Hence the term "integrated", since its function is to coordinate different media and channels to transmit an idea appropriately to the market the company wishes to impact.

Working jointly with the managers and department heads, we did an evaluation of the company's communication channels while measuring response levels.

In the analysis and evaluation, some elements the company already possessed were modified and others were proposed in order to reinforce existing ones, seeking to better define the company's communication objectives and creating better cohesion to better impact customers.

A Comprehensive Communications Plan is a necessity for companies, organizations, or in this case, for E.J.K. Chemical, S.A. de C.V., since the plan can generate innovative proposals that facilitate interaction between the organization, its internal and external audiences.

3.2 THE SALES COMMUNICATION PROCESS

3.2.1 SALES COMMUNICATION

Communication is the verbal or non-verbal transmission of information between someone who wants to express an idea and someone who hopes to capture it or is expected to capture it. Since promotion is a form of communication, we can learn a lot about how to structure effective promotion by examining the communication process. Fundamentally, communication requires only five elements: a message, a message source, a communication channel, a code and a receiver. In practice, however, important additional components come into play (William J. Stanton, Michael J. Etzel, Bruce J. Walker, 2007).

In sales communication, no reference is made exclusively to the ability of salespeople to present ideas to customers, since salespeople's work would have a purely informative function, the transmission of characteristics, and of course, this is not the main objective of sales communication. Their purpose is to successfully complete sales, which inevitably requires an exchange of ideas to meet customers' needs, respond to their objections and determine if customers have received and understood messages.

The objective of sales communication is reached if the client receives, understands and accepts the message. This is perceived through the interest shown by the customer. The following elements make up the communication process:

1. Transmitter: The person who initiates the process, who transmits the message or information. Not only does he or she initiate the message, he or she must also establish the target audience he or she intends to reach with the message.
2. Recipient: The person to whom the message sent by the sender is addressed.
3. Content: The message one wishes to convey, which generally coincides with the sales pitch.
4. Code: Different forms and styles the salesperson uses when transmitting a message. It is a system of interrelated signals, norms or symbols which serve to articulate and transmit the message in a way that is understandable to both the sender and receiver.
5. Channel: The physical medium through which the encoded message is channeled.
6. Feedback: The variable that measures the effectiveness of the communication process. The receiver's response indicates that communication has been effective, when the sender becomes the receiver and vice versa.

There are three important elements within the communicative process:

1. Objectives: what is the intent of the transmission?
   - Immediate objective: obtain clear reception of the message.
   - Intermediate objective: correct interpretation of the message.
   - Final objective: achieve the desired response in customer behavior.

2. Message:
   - Informative messages: information must be properly assimilated by the receiver through messages of methodological organization: the aim is to plan and order the communicative process.
   - Normative messages: intended to guide the receiver's behavior within a model previously determined by the issuer in order to achieve desired objectives.
   - Socio-effective interaction messages: messages addressed to recipients that aim to help them reach their objectives more easily.
3. Channel:
   - The most appropriate channel for the subject to whom it is addressed for the content of the message and the desired objective.
   - The one with the greatest impact.
   - The one that impacts the issuer.

3.2.2 Consumer Profile

3.2.2.1 Consumer Behavior

We define consumer behavior as that which consumers exhibit to find, buy, use, evaluate and discard products and services they expect to meet their needs.

Consumer behavior focuses on the way consumers, families or households make decisions to spend their available resources (time, money, effort) on consumer-related items. This includes what they buy, why they buy it, when, where, how often they buy it, how often they use it, how they evaluate it after purchase, the effect of these evaluations on future purchases, and how they discard it. While all consumers are unique, one of the most important constants among all of us, despite our differences, is that we are all consumers. We use or consume food, clothing, shelter, transportation, education, equipment, vacations, basic needs, luxuries, services and even ideas.

In its broadest sense, consumer behavior describes two different types of consumer entities: the personal consumer and the organizational consumer. Personal consumers buy goods and services for their own use, for their home or as a gift for a third party. In each of these contexts, products are purchased for the final use of individuals, whom we will refer to as final users or final consumers. The second category of consumers, organizational consumers, includes for-profit and non-profit businesses, government agencies (local, state and national) and institutions (for example, schools, hospitals and prisons). They must buy products, equipment and services to run their organizations (Leon G. Schiffman, Leslie Lazar Kanuk, 2010).

3.2.2.2 Consumer profile

A consumer profile is the set of characteristics that, based on analysis of the variables of a market, describes the target customer.

The consumer profile is a tool that, among others, allows the company to:

a) Know and understand their customers.
b) Offer them the products and services they really demand.
c) Develop sales strategies focused on characteristics defined in the profile.
d) Establish channels through which they can contact potential customers.
e) More effectively identify their competitors (Marketing, 2002).

Some characteristics of the consumer profile, which must be determined through consumer research and purchasing analysis, are:

1. Demographic characteristics

Pastimes and interests are based on the age, education and income of individuals, as well as the media to which they are exposed.

Demographic information is the easiest and most logical way to classify individuals and it can be measured more accurately than other bases for segmentation. Demographic data offers the most efficient resource in terms of cost to locate and reach out to specific segments, since most secondary data that is compiled on a population is based on demographic information. Demographic data allows companies to identify business opportunities favored by changes in the age, income or geographical residence of people. Many consumer habits, attitudes and patterns of exposure to the media are directly related to demographic data.

2. Lifestyle

Lifestyle refers to the general pattern of a person's life, including how they invest their time, energy and money. Lifestyles, also known as psychographic data, consist of activities, interests and opinions (AIO). Interests and opinions are cognitive constructs that can be measured through surveys, in which respondents are asked to indicate their level of agreement or disagreement with statements. Some factors examined are similar to personality traits; others include measures of reasons for purchases, attitudes, beliefs and values.

Demographic data determines consumer needs for products and the ability to buy them; psychographic data explains the purchasing decisions of individuals and the choices they make within the purchase options available to them.

3. Motivations

This is the purpose that a customer has when acquiring a product or service. Motivation is defined as the driving force in individuals that pushes them into action. This driving force is generated by a state of tension that exists as a result of an unmet need. Individuals strive both consciously and subconsciously to reduce this tension by choosing methods and using behavior that, according to their expectations, will satisfy their needs and alleviate their stress. These reasons are: physiological, safety, belonging, self-esteem and personal fulfillment.

4. Personality

This reflects the enduring reaction trends of an individual. When asked directly, individuals are unlikely to reveal their personality traits because they are reserved or because they do not consciously recognize them. However, through personality tests, generally in the form of questions or statements presented to the interviewee, researchers are able to determine the personality of an individual.

5. Values

They are the result of the consumer's interaction with the environment in which he or she has lived. These are very important feelings about how good or bad it is to carry out an activity or achieve an objective.

6. Beliefs and attitudes

Thanks to their own experiences or those of others, individuals develop opinions or judgments they consider true, called beliefs. Attitudes are feelings of like or dislike towards something.

7. Perception

This is the process through which media information is captured, interpreted and recalled. It is one of the reasons why people react differently to a stimulus.

8. Learning

This refers to changes that shape, through experience, what consumers believe, their attitudes and behaviors. Consumers can learn in three ways: reward by experience, repeated association and discernment (Marketing, 2002).

3.2.3 PROMOTIONAL MIX

This is the specific mix of promotional tools used by the company to persuasively communicate value to customers and generate relationships with them (Gary Armstrong, Philip Kotler, 2013). Promotion, no matter to who it is directed, is an attempt to influence. It has four forms: personal sales, advertising, sales promotion and public relations.

3.2.3.1 Direct Marketing and Merchandising

3.2.3.1.1 Direct marketing

This refers to the way a product speaks for itself. It is what makes a product sell and it draws the buyer's attention, inspiring feelings of abundance, power and, to some extent, purchase euphoria.

It is a communication process which, through different means or tools, provokes an immediate, measurable response reaction. Its main objective is to increase the impact of products or services on its specific field of customers or prospects in order to boost sales.

Direct marketing is the communication technique with the strongest development globally. Its growth and evolution are due to changes in information technology and telecommunications, the market, consumers and financial pressure on marketers to generate profits amid strong competition. The reasons for using direct marketing are: to reach objectives without depending on others; to test, refine, direct, track and sequence optimal promotional messages; to employ fully measurable, data-driven marketing, to identify and address prospects and convert them into customers.

Through direct marketing tools, companies immediately contact potential consumers. One central element of this strategy is databases with personal information of clients and prospects in the market segment that one wishes to target. The minimum information one should have concerning consumers is their name, address, telephone number, email address, date of birth, interests, income, properties, consumption habits, information about their work and family activity. All of this allows one to clearly define if the person meets the consumer profile one wishes to target.

3.2.3.1.2 Merchandising

This is a set of marketing techniques to maximize profitability of points of sale. This is a key element, so the presentation of products in the establishment will be of the utmost importance.

This promotion tool entails the design of points of sale to achieve maximum profitability through the correct display of the goods it sells; it applies to all perishable or non-perishable products. Before merchandising was defined as a set of techniques, it could be done intuitively: merchants correctly used their experience to improve profitability of their point of sale. Currently, products compete amongst themselves and producers and distributors fight to place them in preferred locations. Since over 50 percent of purchases are decided at the point of sale, the attractiveness of a product is key to achieving a greater number of sales. Part of that capacity depends on its location. "Consumer freedom" in the market is relative; it is not synonymous with manipulation or deception, but rather a series of conditions that induce consumer choice before entering the establishment, such as advertising and image, and when it comes into contact with the point of sale, merchandising techniques.

According to the marketing expert Kepner, merchandising must comply with five fundamental principles:

- Having the right product, that is, an assortment of quality and number, for example, a clothing store should have a variety of sizes and models.
- Having the right amount of product, which refers to good inventory management, for example, in the Christmas season, a supermarket should have a sufficient stock of turkeys for Christmas dinner.

- Having the right price, without forgetting factors such as profitability. If a fair price for a product is determined with which a constant flow of sales is generated, it must be maintained for consumers.
- Taking into account the right time to offer a product. For example, a store that sells ice cream should reduce its amount of ice cream in winter and increase that of other products such as cakes and hot drinks that compensate for the drop in sales during those months.

Finally, the right place to present the product. Supermarkets and department stores have successfully developed this concept, placing basic necessities at the back of stores so consumers can see other products they had not planned to buy and consume them. In aisles, the most popular items are placed in the middle so that people buy other products in order to get to the ones they need. In Mexico, the Federal Consumer Institute recommends that shoppers carry a list of the products they need and only the money they usually spend for these goods, otherwise they will come out with a bill that 50 percent higher than what they planned to spend.

3.2.3.2 Public relations

The company is an element of the environment which is influenced by and influences society. Unfortunately, this influence undergoes unwanted impacts by certain social groups who reject the organization, its products and services. The last few decades of globalization, attention to international markets, the emergence of ecological defense groups, consumers and religious fundamentalist groups have turned public relations into a field with recognizable practices, techniques, skills and limits; it is a strategic resource which institutions cannot do without unless they are willing to risk not having the support of public opinion. Its objective is to establish forms of interaction with the public which foster favorable publicity and a positive image of the company.

Public relations are very credible: news, appearances, sponsorships and events seem more real and credible to readers than ads. Public relations can also reach potential customers who avoid salespeople and advertisements; the message reaches buyers as "news" instead of sales communications. As with advertising, public relations can enhance companies or products. Marketers tend to underuse public relations or use them as last-minute solutions. However, a well-planned public relations campaign used with other elements of the marketing mix can be both effective and economical.

PR departments can perform any or all of the following functions:

- Press relations or press agency: create and place information of journalistic interest in the news media to attract attention to people, products or services.
- Product publicity: generate unpaid advertising of specific products.
- Public affairs: build and maintain relations with the local or national community.
- Investor relations: maintain relationships with shareholders and others in the financial community.
- Development: work with donors or members of non-profit organizations to obtain financial or volunteer support.

3.2.3.3 Advertising

3.2.3.3.1 Background

Advertising goes back to the beginning of recorded history. Archeologists working in countries around the Mediterranean have unearthed posters announcing various events and offers. The Romans painted walls to advertise gladiator fights and the Phoenicians painted paintings on large rocks to promote products along parade routes. During the Golden Age in Greece, town criers announced the sale of livestock, handicrafts and even cosmetics. An ancient "sung commercial" read as follows: "For eyes that shine, for cheeks like the dawn/For beauty that lasts after the youth is gone/For reasonable prices, for the woman who knows/Will buy her cosmetics from Aesclyptos."

Advertising concept

The American Marketing Association (AMA) defines advertising as an impersonal, massive form of dissemination of information, ideas, goods and services, paid for by an identified sponsor, generally using mass media.

Advertising strategy

Advertising strategy consists of two main elements: creating advertising messages and selecting advertising media. In the past, companies often viewed media planning as secondary to the process of creating messages. After the creative department had created ads, the media department selected and acquired the best means to bring those ads to the desired target audiences. This often caused friction between creative staff and media planners (Gary Armstrong, Philip Kotler, 2013).

3.3 CASE STUDY

3.3.1 BACKGROUND

The study of Organizational Communication can be included within the field of social sciences. It has been studied for three decades by recognized theorists.

The leading authors are Joan Costa, Justo Villafañe and José Luis Piñuel from Europe; Charles Redding and Linda Putnam from the U.S. and Carlos Fernández Collado, Rafael Serrano, María Luis Muriel and Carmen Rota from Brazil, Mexico and Argentina.

This important area of communication is known by different names. While much has been done to reinforce its short history as a professional activity, there is still a lot to be done.

3.3.2 METHODOLOGY

Most successful companies locally, regionally or globally recognize the need to establish organizational communication departments, obtaining positive results and contributing to better development of their companies. But as in any business activity, it is always possible to develop an Integral Communication Plan. Some organizations do not have communication plans, so they do not implement them.

This proposal of an Integral Communication Plan for E.J.K. Chemical, S.A. de C.V. is a way to promote its internal and external activities. They can also create programs or activities inside and outside the company based on their own ideas or other proposals.

Based on the previous approach, it should be mentioned that the lack of such a plan has prevented the company from achieving greater visibility locally and nationally. Without communication strategies, promotion and other activities, the relationship and interaction between the company and society is lacking. Indeed, the scope of this initiative is broad and diverse, allowing us to involve the company's internal and external audiences.

Working with digital tools for the promotion of the company involves methodology, and this chapter briefly covers this topic. The main bases are observation, analysis and informal conversations as a qualitative research method.

3.3.2.1 Methodology of the Analysis of E.J.K. Chemical, S.A.

The main purpose being to maintain a direct relationship with the managers and department heads of E.J.K. Químicos, S.A. de C.V, as well as its customers, we needed to perform field research using observation to gather the necessary information and propose strategies as part of the Integral Communication Plan.

3.3.2.2 Population and Sample

The E.J.K. Chemical, S.A. de C.V. team will provide important information for generating the Plan. The group will also include opinions from external clients since they represent a vital part of the business activity.

As for the sample, a selection will be made based on the criteria of the managers and department heads according to certain characteristics. They will then determine the direct and indirect stakeholders who could provide relevant information for development of the Plan.

3.3.2.3 Research Method

Deductive method: We will start by identifying the problems and successes of E.J.K. Químicos, S.A. de C.V.

Analytical method: This method will allow us to identify the situation of the company to implement positive actions by evaluating the main inside and outside effects.

3.3.2.4 Techniques and Tools for Collecting Information

Primary sources

Direct observation: Through this technique, we will maintain direct contact with the people to be investigated, in this case, with customers who purchase products from the company, contrasting them with competing companies.

Consult experts: This type of consultation will be a vital guide for the development and implementation of the proposed plan.

We will conduct interviews with staff, clients and suppliers to learn about their opinions regarding communication between the company and them, as well as the opinions of people who have never bought the company's products, to learn what is needed to gain their preference.

Secondary Sources

<u>Books:</u> Specialized works which lend theoretical support to the information collected.

<u>Publications</u>: All of the documents related to the topic will be taken into account so that the proposal will have professional support.

<u>Internet:</u> Besides being a tool to obtain information, it grants us accessibility to documents that cannot be consulted in libraries or periodicals.

3.3.2.5 Analysis and data processing techniques

Research will be carried out using a qualitative model, because when collecting data, we will analyze subjective information. This will be interpreted according to interviewees' body language, helping us better understand the data collected.

3.3.3 ANALYSIS OF THE SITUATION OF E.J.K. CHEMICAL, S.A. DE C.V.

To identify the main problems that affect the company, a brief study was developed through observation and interviews, allowing us to address both internal and external clients.

The observation and interviews with internal clients focused on the company in general, the General Manager, the company's development and its internal relations.

External customers evaluated their level of satisfaction with respect to the products and strategies implemented by the company as good, fair, satisfactory or poor. We were also able to identify the perception other external customers have, such as suppliers and how the company communicates with them, since they ensure that the products offered by the company to its customers are provided in a timely manner.

3.3.3.1 The company

E.J.K. Chemical, S.A. de C.V., located at Buenos Aires 122, Col. Tetela, Santa Ana Chiautempan, Tlax. C.P. 90810, is a leader in solvent distribution, committed to the environment and dedicated to developing specialty chemical products.

The company is dedicated to the distribution and sales of chemical products for industry, waste water treatment, chemical specialties and the manufacturing of cleaning products, polymers and solvents.

3.3.3.2 Main customers

E.J.K. Chemical, S.A. de C.V. reaches its customers through three different distribution channels: industrial distribution, in which companies provide products that are part of the manufacturing process of a final product; intermediate distribution, in which companies sell products to clients who later resell them in establishments or itinerantly, and direct distribution to customers who buy products for their own use (the last two are common in the cleaning products department).

E.J.K. Chemical, S.A. de C.V. is a growing company that has customers in Tlaxcala and it has also established partnerships with companies in the states of Aguascalientes, San Luis Potosi, Veracruz, Puebla and the State of Mexico.

3.3.3.3 Main suppliers

Fig. 7. Model of the motivation process

3.3.4 Analysis and Diagnosis of Communications at E.J.K. Chemical, S.A. de C.V.

3.3.4.1 Internal Clients

Most workers believe there is an adequate relationship between management and employees, but some said it could be improved in the communication channels based on the information they receive.

- Through observation and interviews, several needs were detected.
- It is essential to provide more information to workers on the mission, vision, objectives and values of the company; this can be achieved through training (induction) and an organizational manual
- In the induction courses, it is important to show workers where different departments are, allowing them to get to know other workers' locations and responsibilities, encouraging mutual support.
- It is important to assign positions according to the training, performance and skills of each staff member. This improves workers' experiences and allows them to demonstrate and apply the knowledge they obtain in their training.

It is important to inform employees of the benefits of the existing internal communication channel.

Human value is important for all departments and their processes, and it defines the success of the company. Therefore, to achieve better worker and company satisfaction, job training and human motivation should be a priority.

3.3.4.2 The General Manager

The general manager must inform internal and external audiences, along with department heads, of decisions made at the managerial level through circulars, and listen to opinions and suggestions that can contribute positively.

To achieve improvement, the director should assign tasks and give feedback. If a worker does a good job, the director should express satisfaction with the work done. In addition to assessing work, this will generate greater commitment, or at least serve as a benchmark to improve next time.

3.3.4.3 Organizational development

It is important that the company, when hiring employees, informs them of the benefits offered by the company. To increase their interest, it is essential to let them know that they will develop as collaborators of the company and that they will receive the training they need to strengthen and expand their skills in order to help them meet the company's objectives and their professional and personal goals.

Some areas where it is necessary to assist staff with their work and personal lives are:

- Technological advances.
- Management of social networks.
- Human relations.
- First aid.

3.3.4.4 Work

The workers at E.J.K. Chemical, S.A. de C.V. have a favorable opinion of the work they do. However, one of the difficulties with the company's internal public is that, as previously mentioned, workers lack training. Another reason is that some details that have become relevant to the institution may have been ignored.

Some of the suggestions on this topic are the following:

- Reinforce motivation.
- Implement communication tools.
- Hold informational meetings.

The staff of E.J.K. Chemical, S.A. de C.V. knows its importance within the company, but recognition, congratulations and developing pride for the work done by workers can improve their satisfaction.

3.3.4.5 External Public

The external public (suppliers, employees' relatives and customers) is very important to public and private companies, who recognize their vital importance in the productive process.

This is why, to better serve them, owners and employees have been involved in both broad and specialized studies of external audiences, using various research methodologies. E.J.K. Chemical, S.A. de C.V. is no exception. We will describe the main conclusions gleaned from observation and interviews.

- Greater communication is needed, using media to publicize the strategies, activities and events in which they are involved and which they benefit from.

3.3.5 Comprehensive Communication Plan

3.3.5.1 Overall Objective

Create communication systems that significantly increase the influx of local and national customers to E.J.K. Chemical, S.A. de C.V.

3.3.5.2 Specific Objectives

- Develop organizational culture through internal communication strategies.
- Execute external communication strategies to increase customers.
- Create methods to evaluate and support the Comprehensive Communication Plan in order to achieve proposed objectives.

3.3.5.3 Justification

The importance of proposing an integral communication plan is to collaborate in improving the communicative relationship with internal and external clients in order to increase the affluence and interest of local and national customers in the products sold by E.J.K. Chemical, S.A. de C.V. The plan will result in better media development and will make effective use of resources, achieving greater benefits. The proposal should establish and define internal and external communication strategies, specifying the process for the detection and formulation of communication needs and the evaluation of the effectiveness of the channels used, so that they may be incorporated in the actions defined in the Communications Plan.

3.3.5.4 SWOT Analysis (Strengths, Weaknesses, Opportunities and Threats)

The SWOT analysis is known for its simplicity in organizational studies and analysis. The SWOT analysis is a tool which allows users to construct a table in which information from studies may be entered, in this case for E.J.K. Chemical, S.A. de C.V. Through the data analyzed, the SWOT gives a clear diagnosis which will facilitate work when the communication strategies based on the objectives we have set are presented.

3.3.5.5 Internal Communication Strategies according to the needs of the Internal and External Clients of E.J.K. Chemical, S.A. de C.V.

3.3.5.5.1 Analysis

It is important to know about the sales and advertising processes of a company in order to perform an analysis of the time elapsed from the moment customers place their orders until the moment of delivery.

Waiting time ranges from 15 to 45 minutes. This varies depending on internal and external factors.

The internal factors are:

- Missing staff
- Product handling errors
- Errors in the issuance of receipts or invoices
- Product spills
- Contingency (oversaturation of orders)

The external factors are:

- Unidentified containers
- Indecision to purchase
- Lack of awareness of the purchasing process
- Weather
- Damaged packaging
- Cancellation or modification of orders by customers

Another important factor is that because of their lack of time during the week, customers tend to buy on Saturdays. Even though the company has expanded its reception and delivery staff, the time problem has not been completely solved.

In its search to make waiting time more enjoyable, the company has implemented:

- A refreshment area, where from 8 a.m. to 11 a.m. customers are given free tea or coffee while waiting for orders; from noon to 4 p.m. they are given a fruit drink.
- A TV for customers to watch.
- Free celebrity magazines.

In the Comprehensive Communication Plan for E.J.K. Chemical, S.A. de C.V., some elements were implemented and modified to correctly optimize company resources.

3.3.5.5.2 Television Programming

The implementation of a program through which the company broadcasts to customers new, different content, broadcasting information the company wishes to share with its customers as well as philosophical and general interest videos.

3.3.5.5.3 Design Of A New Company Website

One of the integral communication strategies modified for the company was redesigning its website.

3.3.5.5.4 Design Of Identifiers For Product Containers

To better position the brand in the consumer's mind and as part of integral communications, we sought to implement advertising material that would be useful to the customer while helping sell products. Previously, when customers purchased products their packaging was identified with the name of the customer and the product they wanted. This was done by sticking a label with tape with the customer's information. This process was modified.

3.3.5.5.5 Modification And Implementation Of New Promotions

The cleaning products manufactured and sold by the company must have attractive promotion that provides identity and market presence. This is why another task in the implementation of the integral marketing communication plan was to observe and analyze the promotion of each product to improve and implement promotions for products that did not have one yet.

3.3.5.5.6 Implementation Of A New Product Catalog

The product catalog is one of the fundamental parts of communications. It is a printed medium that is in constant interaction with the customer. Similarly, to the company website, we evaluated and analyzed the current product catalog. Many important elements were highlighted.

3.3.6 Results

3.3.6.1 Company Video

Undoubtedly, the most important objective of making a company video is to broadcast its brand image. Building and strengthening the company's brand image should be a long-term objective for all corporations.

The company video that was created will be a perfect support for customers to watch, while broadcasting a set of values to the target audience. The audience will stop considering the company as a "thing" or lifeless entity and begin to humanize it, value it and feel empathy for it. The contents of the video were compiled over a four-month period, with images of products, employees and manufacturing workstations.

3.3.6.2 Website

On the website, several improvements were made, such as:

- Shortening banner load time.
- Improving programming.
- Improving image quality.
- Redistributing information contained in the webpage.
- Updating information.

3.3.6.3 Redesigning Product Labels

The label is a fundamental part of a product. It identifies, describes and differentiates, informs the customer, and of course, complies with the laws and regulations of the industry or sector.

We analyzed the current labels, and encouraged the company to redesign certain labels in order to make some products more easily identifiable for customers.

3.3.6.4 Product Catalog

The catalog we designed for the company after analyzing its current offerings will be a useful tool to promote the company's products.

3.4 REFERENCES

Cooperativa, L. (20 de 1 de 2009). Loria Cooperativa. Obtenido de Loria Cooperativa: http://dgpcfadu.com.ar/2009/1_cuat/ v20/tp/ayuda_glosario.html

Gary Armstrong, Philip Kotler. (2013). Fundamentos de marketing. México: Person.

Leon G. Schiffman, Leslie Lazar Kanuk. (2010). Comportamiento del consumidor. México : Pearson.

Marketing. (25 de 11 de 2002). Gestiopolis. Obtenido de Gestiopolis: https://www.gestiopolis.com/que-es-un-perfil-del-consumidor/

Promocion. (s.f.). Documentos Merca. Obtenido de Documentos Merca: file:///C:/Users/Cliente%202/Downloads/Documents/Merca%205a_Unidad9.pdf

William J. Stanton, Michael J. Etzel, Bruce J. Walker. (2007). Fundamentos de Marketing. Mexico: McGraw Hill.

CHAPTER IV

Innovation Focused on the Agro-industrial Sector

José Luis Méndez Hernández, Clara Romero Cruz, Roberto Vega Rocha, Laura Gutiérrez López.

Abstract The following article focuses on a review of the scientific literature on agro-industrial innovation to evaluate the current state of this concept worldwide. We performed this review using scientific platforms such as Thomson Reuters, gathering scientific literature from 2013 to 2017. We also evaluated the degree of impact of the journals where the articles were published. We found that different elements intervene in the creation of innovative agro-industrial companies, including intellectual capital, culture, business cooperation, institutional frameworks, innovative behavior, business and market orientation, university-industry relations, vocational training centers, entrepreneurial orientation, geographical concentration and technological capacity. We detected a knowledge management model focused on the agro-industrial sector; however, it does not take into account the previously mentioned elements in the structure of the model.

Keywords: Agroindustry, Innovation, Competitiveness

71

4.1 INTRODUCTION

A great deal of literature exists on the relevance of competitiveness as a key factor for companies to remain in customers' preference and stay strong in today's increasingly fluctuating markets. Customer preferences continuously change and companies must be flexible in manufacturing, innovation, organization and their business model in order to be competitive. Michael Porter is one of the most iconic writers, and he mentions that the competitiveness of companies in a given country lies in their inherent capacity to innovate and improve in the products and services offered (Porter, 1996).

Porter identifies a relevant factor: the ability to innovate. Innovation is recognized as one of the main drivers of business success and economic development in today's knowledge-based economy. Researchers have found that innovation con-tributes significantly to economic growth since it is the basis for increasing productivity, both through incremental improvements and change of progress (Pavitt, 1969). Innovation is also widely recognized as playing a central role in creating value and maintaining competitive advantages (Jamrog, 2006).

The concept of innovation was initially defined by the economist Schumpeter as "a process of creative destruction, where the search for innovation pushes constantly breaking the old rules to establish new ones, implying the introduction of new products, new processes, the opening of new markets or the introduction of new forms of organization" (Zhen, et al., 2014).

The previous argument leads us to consider the content of the Oslo Manual. Innovation is divided into four major areas: product innovation, consisting of the introduction of a product or service with improvements in its technical characteristics that are appreciated and perceived by consumers; process innovation, focused on the improvement of production or distribution processes; marketing innovation, relating to new marketing methods, and finally, innovation in organization, consisting of the introduction of a new method of organizing the workplace and the external relations of companies (Oslo Manual, 2005).

Companies require skills to acquire and apply innovative knowledge to create new products and services, marketing practices and the opening of new markets, technology and organization of production, forms of organization and business management. They also need to create new ways of relating to business networks and value chains, with providers of business development and financing services, universities and other potential sources of innovative knowledge (Cummings, 2013).

The current context of technological innovation is one of constant change. The generation, access and adaptation of knowledge, coupled with the emergence and accelerated diffusion of new technologies, require permanent adaptation, which constitutes a challenge for society as a whole. Economic and social growth, the maintenance of employment and competitiveness, inevitably go through innovation and technological transfer (Zarazúa, Solleiro et al., 2009).

4.2 JUSTIFICATION

Once the importance of innovation and its different areas have been highlighted, it is important to point out that the present research proposal will focus on studying the agro-industrial sector. This sector, which is important for the vast majority of countries, refers to a social and historical construct, that is, a set of processes and social relationships of production, processing, distribution and consumption of fresh and processed foods in different areas. These arguments highlight the global relevance of the agro-industrial sector, and therefore, the need for this sector to be highly competitive (Ocón, 2015). The main problem identified in our literary review is that until now, scientific research has focused on the study of elements or variables that directly affect the formation of innovative agro-industrial companies. These elements were studied separately, but we believe these elements must be considered as a whole.

4.3 HYPOTHESIS

The main hypothesis is that the agro-industrial sector is currently in an exceptional development phase in developed countries, while in developing countries it is precarious. Therefore, most companies do not have the administrative and operational practices that help form highly competitive global organizations. The objective of our work is a detailed literary review of the subject of agro-industrial innovation, in order to learn more about this highly relevant concept.

4.4 THEORETICAL FRAMEWORK

Competitiveness means the ability to enter a market and position oneself in it. Companies need to have some kind of advantage over potential competitors in price, quality, quantity, opportunity, presentation, packaging, delivery conditions or financing (Corpoica, 2000). To gain competitive advantage, agro-industrial companies collaborate with supply chain partners in knowledge exchange, that is, not only the incorporation of new companies in the sector, but also sustainably to guarantee added value. This context establishes key guidelines to achieve a cycle of technological innovation within the agro-industry. Beyond their strategic intention and organizational structure, agro-industrial companies must establish a set of processes that promote innovation and increase company success. Developing the company's ideology to create innovation in every aspect of the organization requires maximizing benefits and minimizing risks associated with new innovations (Dyer and Singh, 1998). The incorporation of different types of innovation depends on the company's capacity. This capacity is expressed by certain inherent characteristics of the producers, production unit or company and its relationship with the operating environment, to the extent that these characteristics support innovation (Nossal and Lim, 2011). It must also be recognized that the effect or impact of each innovation on the company's performance is different.

The most important, complex issue that an agro-industrial company may face is the simultaneous incorporation of the four types of innovation. This can be seen as a consequence of the fact that innovation in agro-industrial companies tends to be sequential (Nossal and Lim, 2011). The use of technology in the agro-industrial sector has historically served as a mediating tool between man and nature. Its basic function in theory is to contribute substantially to transforming nature for the benefit of people who live in the countryside. In the West, the use of technology has been mentioned in discourse as the axis converting from tradition to modernity (Herrera, 2006). Tradition is supplanted by technological innovation, bringing with it a series of economic and sociocultural situations that many authors have examined in terms of their impacts and implications of social order. Thus, technology is understood as "a set of specific knowledge and processes to transform reality and solve a problem" (Lara, 1998, p. 2). Thus, technology is a key element in the development of the agricultural sector, and it is clearly necessary to increase competitiveness in the face of national and international productive forces. This argument, which typifies innovation in terms of degree of technology, assumes that innovations are not equal depending on the characteristics of the technologies incorporated, the impact and technologies required (Ariza et. al., 2013).

4.5 RESEARCH METHODOLOGY

For the present research proposal, we performed a review of scientific literature, focusing on the topic of innovation in the global agro-industrial sector.

The review was carried out using the Thomson Reuters platform. We first considered the level of impact of the journals containing the articles consulted; most current literature consulted on the subject of study was dated 2013 to 2017. We also considered classic literature on competitiveness and innovation, such as Schumpeter and Porter.

4.6 TYPE OF RESEARCH

This is a descriptive investigation, its intention being to refer to the states, characteristics and phenomena that occur naturally, without explaining the relationships identified between the different factors that determine it. Although it attempts to analyze the relationships between categories (technological strategy and management processes) to determine the behavior of the product, it has no explanatory or correlation claims, that is, it does not seek to find causal relationships between these two elements.

4.7 DEVELOPMENT METHODOLOGY

The authors Aporte, Castilla, Sánchez and Gallardo (2017) identify the characteristics of this type of agro-industry and demonstrate the importance of adopting a responsible orientation in the promotion of reputation to create sustainable competitive advantages. Cognitive-organizational proximity is a positive determinant of business cooperation with other organizations, while social and institutional proximity are negative determinants. They also establish that business cooperation is a positive determinant of business innovation. In addition, it is observed that levels of business cooperation are lower in microenterprises, a result that differs from developed countries. In Geldes, Heredia, Felzensztein and Mora (2017), an institutional framework that legitimizes technological innovations is a condition of success for agro-industrial models through the emergence of new, "innovative" social actors. Gras and Hernández (2016) explain that research proposes and develops the concept of technological complexity (TC) as a useful, simple tool to group key attributes that add value to products (multinomial logistic regression model with mixed effects). According to Cotes A., Muñoz and Cotes, J.M. (2016), innovative companies obtain better results in both economic and productive terms. In addition, the innovative aspect of the agro-industrial sector has been less affected by the economic recession than other economic sectors. In Zouaghi and Sanchez (2016), the principal significant factors of the competitiveness of the agro-industrial sector are identified: geographical concentration, specialization of companies, scope of viable and relevant businesses, privileged position, complementarity through the use of byproducts, cooperation among cluster companies, uniformity of technological level, culture adapted to the cluster, evolution in new technologies and results strategy oriented to the cluster. In Sarturi, Augusto, Vargas, Boaventura and Dos Santos (2016), the authors propose a model to measure the technological capacity of agro-industrial companies, since technological capacity plays an important role in the efficiency of the productive process of companies and their degree of innovation. It is associated with the skills and knowledge needed for companies to absorb, use, adapt, develop and transfer technologies. De Mori, Batalha and Alfranca (2016) identify the first of five dimensions, resources: research intensity, human resources and infrastructure. Mirzaei, Micheels and Boecker (2016) explain technological updating: pre-processing, processing, controls and environmental aspects. Mujeyi, Mutambara, Siziba and Sadomba (2015) focus on processes and routines: product engineering, process engineering, monitoring and project management, planning and control. Bitzer and Bijman (2014) write about learning mechanisms: internal and external acquisitions, socialization and coding. Finally, Storer, Hyland, Ferrer, Santa and Griffiths (2014) explore coordination and accessibility: interaction with the environment, relations with suppliers, accessible sources of information and intensity of participation.

Review of scientific literature on agro-industrial innovation leads to the detection of certain problems, including the imbalance in the development of different types of innovation, whereby process innovation is least developed in agro-industrial companies. This is very important because experts in business competitiveness, such as Porter, mention that competitive advantage lies in an organization's processes and internal resources. Furthermore, agro-industrial companies have focused on product innovation. In addition, different elements were detected that are linked to the generation of innovative agro-industrial companies, including: Intellectual capital - Cultural aspects - Business cooperation - Geographical concentration - Institutional framework - Innovative behavior - Technological capacity - Business and market orientation - Technological monitoring - Industry-university relationship - Intellectual capital - Entrepreneurial guidance - Professional training.

The knowledge management model (Pérez and García, 2013) proposes a model for the management of knowledge in the agro-industrial sector, specifically in Colombia's fruit and vegetable industry. The model is based on forming a network that promotes acquisition, production, dissemination and knowledge transfer. It is firmly established that knowledge is placed in the center of such a network.

As such, it is understood that the solution to the problems of agro-industry is not based solely on infrastructure, which, although it is considered necessary and especially biased by the fact that large investments are required, is not the only factor involved in the development of the agro-industrial sector. An additional component is the implementation of the knowledge network, which works to manage shared knowledge through the interdisciplinary work of various actors that strive to obtain benefits for this sector of the agricultural economy.

The model proposed by the authors is the Etzkowitz traditional triple helix model, used as a metaphor to express a dynamic alternative to the model of innovation prevailing in the policies of the 1980s, while visualizing the inherent complexity of innovation processes (Etzkowitz, 2003).

The proposed model consists of three fundamental nodes to characterize the knowledge network in the fruit production chain of the department of Córdoba as a strategy for generating innovation in the sector. These nodes are connected as follows: primary producer node, association node and technological node. These nodes act as points of transfer or interconnection through which knowledge flows. They can be described as storage centers of information that are interconnected systematically, so nodes can be described as a sequence.

Most activity is concentrated on the primary producer node, which generates the primary product as a result of the internal application of acquired knowledge, demonstrating the degree of effectiveness of the proposed strategy. In addition, the evaluation of various events that have occurred becomes a source of valuable information that can be applied to future experiences.

The association node is a repository or central knowledge node in which related experiences are found through problems and their solutions. The way in which knowledge flows and spreads through all components of the network can be established through this node or nucleus, in order to facilitate its effective implementation in the different nodes or components that require its use.

The technological node serves as a channel that facilitates and promotes intercommunicative activity between different actors, converting the technological component into a tool that facilitates the implementation and development of multiple possibilities. This shows how ideas, whether positive or negative, can be accessed or disseminated.

The model also includes what the authors call facilitating agents. The goal is for these elements to stimulate the performance of staff and accelerate operative processes. Considering their direct impact on organizations, these elements are classified as external facilitators related to market conditions, cultural factors and sectoral elements, providing elements for the regulation or management of agro-industrial activities. These components constitute the environment of this sector, and as such its dynamics directly influence it.

The external facilitating agents described in our proposed model are markets, knowledge, strategy and self-management. The internal facilitators of the internal management of the supply chain are an inherent part of the production system and supply chain during the harvesting and post-harvesting stages, and they are involved with the principal node or core. Internal facilitators are the disease prevention program and the system of access to new markets and expansion in new environments. In this proposed model, each node is associated with a facilitating agent but there is no obligation to associate them with others based on the desired strategy. Internal facilitators of primary nodes are: quality of tools implemented, quality of knowledge, productivity, teaching, workshops and conferences. Meanwhile, internal facilitators of the association node include performance of associations, modernization and continuous improvement. Finally, the internal facilitators of the technological node are implementation of technology and technical innovation.

The model also has several indicators established throughout the network which allow each event in a specific area to be monitored and registered. In turn, the necessary corrections or adjustments of a specific performance can be made as required based on specific arguments and specific reasons, facilitating the management and control of the entire network.

4.8 CONCLUSIONS

The latest contributions to the topic of agro-industrial innovation argue that different elements seek to generate innovation and with it the management of robust companies in a competitive context, including: intellectual capital, cultural aspects, business cooperation, geographical concentration, institutional frameworks, innovative behavior, technological capacity, business and market orientation, technological monitoring, industry-university relationship, intellectual capital, entrepreneurial orientation and vocational training centers.

Scientific research so far is limited to analyzing each of these elements individually. This creates a need for new research that would determine whether these elements can work together towards an innovation management model specific to the agro-industrial sector to empower innovation in this economic sector. The knowledge management model proposed by Pérez and Garcia (2013) contributes considerably to the subject of agro-industrial innovation, but it does not include the most recent elements in the formation of innovative organizations. Therefore, new research on this topic would be highly relevant.

4.9 REFERENCES

Castilla Polo, Francisca; Isabel Sanchez Hernandez, M.; Gallardo Vazquez, Dolores. Assessing the Influence of Social Responsibility on Reputation: An Empirical Case-Study in Agricultural Cooperatives in Spain. Journal of Agricultural & Environmental ethics Volume: 30 Issue: 1 Pages: 99-120 Published: Febrero 2017.

César Ariza, Laura Rugeles, Diana Saavedra and Bladimir Guaitero (2013). Meas-uring Innovation in Agricultural Firms: A Methodological Approach. Electronic Journal of Knowledge Management. 11(3). 2/3.

Cotes-Torres, Alejandro; Antonio Munoz-Gallego, Pablo; Miguel Cotes-Torres, Jose. Technological complexity: a tool for understanding the behaviour of consumers of high value-added foodstuffs. Journal of Business Economics and Management Volume: 17 Issue: 3 Pages: 444-457 Published: JUN 2016.

Cummings, A. (2013). Construyendo capacidades de innovación en iniciativas asociativas de pequeñas agroindustrias rurales en El Salvador. Revista Iberoamericana de Ciencia, Tecnología y Sociedad - CTS, Septiembre, 295-319.

De Oslo, M. (2005). Guía para la recogida e interpretación de datos sobre inno-vación. Luxembourg: OECD.

De Mori, Claudia; Batalha, Mario Otavio; Alfranca, Oscar. A model for measuring technology capability in the agrifood industry companies. British Food Journal Volume: 118 Issue: 6 Pages: 1422-1461 Published: 2016.

Gras, Carla; Hernández, Valeria. Custom farming and its integration into the agro-business model: production and services in the Pampa región. Mundo Agrario Volume: 17 Issue: 36 Article Number: e028 Published: DEC 2016.

Geldes, Cristian; Heredia, Jorge; Felzensztein, Christian; et al. Proximity as deter-minant of business cooperation for technological and non-technological in-novations: a study of an agribusiness cluster. Journal of Business & Indus-trial Marketing Volume: 32 Issue: 1 Pages: 168-179 Published: 2017.

Mirzaei, Omid; Micheels, Eric T.; Boecker, Andreas. Product and Marketing Inno-vation in Farm-Based Businesses: The Role of Entrepreneurial Orientation and Market Orientation International Food and Agribusiness Management Review Volume: 19 Issue: 2 Pages: 99-129 Published: 2016.

Ocón, h. b. f. (2015). cadenas, redes y actores de la agroindustria en el contexto de la globalización. el aporte de los enfoques contemporáneos del desarrollo regional. espiral. estudios sobre estado y sociedad, 13(37).

Pérez Pérez, Mario F, Medina García, Victor H (2013) Knowledge Management Model for Fruit-Horticultural Agroindustry Case: Córdoba - Colombia International Journal of Future Computer and Communication.

Sarturi, Greici; Augusto, Carlos; Vargas, Franca; et al. Competitiveness of clusters: A comparative analysis between wine industries in Chile and Brazil. Inter-national Journal of Emerging Markets Volume: 11 Issue: 2 Special Is-sue: SI Pages: 190-213 Published: 2016.

Storer, Maree; Hyland, Paul; Ferrer, Mario; et al. Strategic supply chain manage-ment factors influencing agribusiness innovation utilization. International Journal of Logistics Management Volume: 25 Issue: 3 Pages: 487-521 Published: 2014.

Zarazúa, J. A., Solleiro, J. L., Altamirano, C. R., Castañón, I. R., y Rendón M. R., (2009). Esquemas de innovación tecnológica y su transferencia en las agroempresas frutícolas del estado de Michoacán. Estudios sociales (Her-mosillo, Son.), 17(34), 37-71.

Zouaghi, Ferdaous; Sanchez, Mercedes. Capturing value from alliance portfolio diversity: The mediating role of R&D human capital in high and low tech industries.

Zhen Liu, Ron G.M. Kemp, Maarten A. Jongsmac, Caicheng Huangd, J.J.M. (Hans) Dons and S.W.F Omtaf (2014). Key Success Factors of Innovation Pro-jects of Vegetable Breeding Companies in China. International Food and Agribusiness Management Review. 17(4).

DIGITAL BIBLIOGRAPHY:

Herrera Tapia, Francisco. (2006). Innovaciones tecnológicas en la agricultura em-presarial mexicana: Una aproximación teórica. Gaceta Laboral, 12(1), 93-119. Recuperado en 21 de junio de 2016, de http://goo.gl/id40jo.

BOOKS:

CORPOICA (Corporación Colombiana de Investigación Agropecuaria) (2000). Lecturas sobre economía campesina y desarrollo tecnológico. Co-lombia.
Porter, M.E. (1980) Competitive Strategy. Techniques for Analyzing Industries and Competitors, The Free Press, New York.

CHAPTER V

Implementation of Corporate Financing Projects in The Trade Sector: A Case Study

Esmeralda Aguilar Pérez, Katia Lorena Avilés Coyoli, Sergio Hernández Corona, Romualdo Martínez Carmona.

Abstract: Issues arising from organizational management are some of the most important challenges for companies in the trade sector. This is due to not implementing actions to make financing more efficient and allow liquidity to stimulate growth. The purpose of our study was to analyze if the implementation of financing projects improves competitiveness of companies in the trade sector of the south-central region of Mexico. The study was conducted using data from the Mexican Business Information System published in March 2018, with a sample of 165 companies. From the results obtained, we concluded that implementation of financing projects is directly related to the competitiveness of companies, since 67.9 % of companies have implemented financing projects and 32.1% of companies have not.

Keywords: Financing project, Trade sector, Competitiveness.

5.1 INTRODUCTION

Companies in the trade sector are created by one or several people endowed with a strong capacity for effort, vocation, intuition and vision to develop and implement a business plan, to which they devote their energy and dedication (Pérez and Gilbert, 2012). Business owners seek to transmit their companies to their descendants, but only a small portion of companies manages to reach the second generation (Corona, Gómez and Gómez, 2016).

In 2016, the Organization for Economic Cooperation and Development (OECD) stated that one of the problems affecting trade sector economies in emerging countries is the failure to implement financing projects that could reverse the negative effects of the social and economic inequality of inhabitants of these countries. The OECD position is symptomatic: it reflects a clear rejection of the possible pretension of circumscribing the concept of development to a single economic dimension. However, in most emerging economies, government programs strengthen the Human Development Index (HDI) through entrepreneurship and business development programs. Governments encourage entrepreneurs, small and medium-sized businesses to be more competitive.

In a study carried out in 2012 on a sample of companies in the global trade sector, of 100 companies, only 33 were passed on from the first to the second generation, and of these 33 companies, only 15 passed on to the third generation (Pérez and Gilbert, 2012). The disappearance of these companies is directly related to the lack of proper use of financing, resulting in lack of liquidity to continue operating (Salgado, 2016).

The trade sector is a fundamental part of the productive structures of both industrialized and developing economies (Muñoz, Salgado and Rogela, 2014). Trade sector companies play a determining role in the generation of national wealth, although they are often little-known productive structures. Therefore, research on trade sector companies is of global interest. (Hernández, Marín, Del Valle and Castillo, 2015).

According to data from the National Institute of Statistics and Geography (INEGI), the latest economic census shows that 90 percent of Mexican SMEs are trade sector companies (INEGI, 2016). The leadership of trade-based businesses in the Mexican economic fabric is evident. In statistical terms, it has been proven that, both in our country and worldwide, these companies play a fundamental role in the creation of wealth and employment. The United Nations Development Program (UNDP), in collaboration with the Mexican trade sector enterprise institute, groups together 100 leading companies in their sectors, with an average annual turnover of 1 billion euros. These figures show the involvement of the trade sector in economic activity (UNDP, 2015).

Therefore, it is essential for the different levels of government to join forces to more strictly control support for financing projects. Around 50 percent of these projects fail because they are not followed up on, or because beneficiaries fail to comply with requirements (Romero, 2016). The resources accessed by beneficiaries are only those of the first stage, but by failing to comply with requirements, they no longer qualify for the second stage of the project (Domínguez, 2014).

5.2 BACKGROUND

This section deals with financing projects, their components and their implementation. The term financing projects is defined as a technical and economic proposal to solve a social problem using human, material and technological resources through a written document which includes a series of studies that allow investors to know if their projects materialize (Escudero, 2004). Baca (2013) defines a productive project as a plan that, if a certain amount of capital is assigned and various types of supplies are provided, produces a good or service useful to society. The Inter-American Development Bank (IDB), through the Multilateral Investment Fund (MIF), defines financing projects as those whose objective is to improve the competitiveness of a defined group of small-scale, sector-based, geographically concentrated companies through collective actions.

Generally speaking, Financing Projects include three main components: 1. Strengthening cooperative relations, 2. Reorganization of the production mode and 3. Productive specialization (IDB, 2014).

Regarding the implementation of financing projects, Cárdenas (2013) in Peru determined that the implementation of financing projects increases the production of goods or services. García and Piña (2013) in Venezuela analyzed the valuation of productive investments in order to determine the creation of financial and intellectual value. Similarly, Álvarez (2013) carried out a study of companies in the trade sector in Honduras to determine their link to development. Carrión, Zula and Castillo (2016) analyzed management strategy in small and medium-sized businesses and the application of financing projects in the catering industry in Ecuador.

Martínez (2012) in Chile analyzed micro-financing strategies to overcome poverty, boost the economy, promote self-employment and employment in general. He also analyzed financial education, which enables the adequate of use of cash and microloans and the proper management of personal microfinance. Aguilar, Pinzón and Duran (2015), studied the implications of textile maquiladora financing projects for rural women in Yucatán, Mexico. In addition, Kú, et al., (2013) evaluated locally sustainable financing projects in Calakmul, Mexico, to determine how these projects are self-sustaining. Ramirez, Pérez and Hernández (2013) analyzed the financing projects supported by the 3x1 Program for Migrants from 2007 to 2011 in Zacatecas in order to identify the municipalities and communities where they are located, the legal framework for their business activities and the way their operations are organized.

In another study carried out by Reyes and Pacheco (2014), two experiences of financing projects in the states of Oaxaca and Yucatán are analyzed, comparing the way in which men and women face adverse situations such as recession, migration and marginalization.

5.3. THEORETICAL FRAMEWORK

5.3.1. Strategies of companies in the trade sector

Currently, a strategy is being developed that can be implemented in companies in the trade sector, combining those developed in Mexico, Bolivia, Colombia and the United States. Such is the strategy developed by Valenzuela, Vázquez, Burgueño and Guillén (2016), proposing a professionalization strategy to improve the competitiveness of companies in the trade sector. Meanwhile, Goyzueía (2013) developed a management strategy for companies in the trade sector with prospects for growth and sustainability. Likewise, Botero, Giraldo and Ceballos (2016) designed a Modernization strategy for the Management of Organizations (MMGO). Pukall and Calabrò (2013) designed an integration strategy and a critical examination of the internationalization of companies in the trade sector. Similarly, Gómez, et al. (2014) implemented a behavioral agency strategy and a review of investments in research and development of companies in the trade sector. Finally, Vargas, Pérez and Andrés (2016) developed a financing strategy that applies to companies in the trade sector.

In different countries, studies are being conducted to develop strategies that will enable companies in the trade sector to continue to operate and contribute to their competitiveness. However, the most serious difficulties for companies in the trade sector result from inappropriate use of company financial resources. This causes organizational malfunction, which can result in lack of liquidity, leading to little or no growth. It is also very easy to confuse the flows of the trade and professional sector, which is displayed in demotivation, lack of growth and problems related to successions: selection of the leader and resistance to change (Molina and Gilbert, 2015).

Other authors have suggested that trade companies should design strategies that implement financing projects as a form of financing or liquidity (Desyllas and Sako, 2013). For companies in the trade sector to become more competitive and keep pace with the market, they must support themselves through adequate financial management

(Xi, Kraus, Filser and Kellermanns, 2015), which is necessary to expand their opportunities and increase their capital through associations or mergers with external stakeholders. These options are based on strategic alliances, joint ventures, mergers, takeovers or other forms of collaboration (Wach and Wojciechowski, 2014).

5.3.2 FINANCING PROJECTS

In order to identify the countries that are developing research on the implementation of financing projects, we identified the author, the year of the study, the country where it was applied and the result of the evaluation.

Table 10. Evaluations of financing projects

Authors	Study Country	Project Evaluation of Financing
Carrión, Zula and Castillo (2016).	Ecuador	Analyzed management strategy in small and medium-sized businesses and the application of financing projects in the catering industry in Ecuador.
Aguilar, Pinzón and Duran, (2015)	Mexico	Studied the implications of textile maquiladora financing projects for women in rural areas of Yucatán, Mexico.
Reyes and Pacheco (2014)	Mexico	Analyzed two experiences of financing projects in the states of Oaxaca and Yucatán, comparing the way in which men and women face adverse situations such as recession, migration and marginalization.

As can be seen in Table 10, the pioneering countries performing research regarding the implementation of financing projects are in Latin America. Our main findings allow us to infer that financing allows liquidity, which encourages growth. We thus proceeded to our research project on a strategy related to financing projects implemented in companies in the trade sector.

5.4 GENERAL OBJECTIVE

The objective of this study is to analyze whether the implementation of financing projects improves the competitiveness of companies in the trade sector of the South Central Region of Mexico, which includes the states of Guerrero, Hidalgo, Michoacán, Morelos, Querétaro, Tlaxcala and Puebla.

5.4.1 SPECIFIC OBJECTIVES

- Test through statistical analysis if there is a linear relationship between competitiveness and the implementation of financing projects.
- Test through statistical analysis if the size of the company in the trade sector is a determining factor in its degree of competitiveness.
- Test through statistical analysis if the location in a Mexican state affects the competitiveness of companies.

5.5 METHODOLOGY

For compliance in this research, we defined variables, established a hypothesis and conducted field research, collecting data using a previously validated questionnaire.

5.5.1 RESEARCH SUBJECTS

The profile of the research subjects was directors, managers, partners and owners of businesses in the trade sector in south-central Mexico. In this research project, the participants studied were companies in the trade sector of the south-central region of Mexico. According to the Mexican Business Information System (SIEM), there are 123,338 registered companies that were used as a base. Of these, 45% are involved in trade, 30% in services, and the rest are industrial, as shown in Fig. 8.

State	Total Establishments	Industrial Sector 25%	Services Sector 30%	Commercial Sector 45%
Michoacán	55,228	13807	16568	24853
Puebla	22,767	5692	6830	10245
Querétaro	17,881	4470	5364	8046
Tlaxcala	10,756	2689	3227	4840
Hidalgo	10,710	2678	3213	4820
Guerrero	3,978	995	1193	1790
Morelos	2,018	505	605	908
Totals	123,338	30835	37001	55502

Fig. 8. Composition of companies in the South Central Region of Mexico.

5.5.2 CONCEPTUAL ANALYSIS

In order to confirm that the implementation of financing projects improves the competitiveness of companies in the trade sector of the South Central Region of Mexico. we determined the linear relationship between competitiveness and financing.

DEPENDENT VARIABLE:

The competitiveness of companies in the trade sector of the south central region of Mexico.

INDEPENDENT VARIABLES:

The implementation of productive projects in companies in the trade sector of the south central region of Mexico.

The size of the company in the trade sector of the south central region of Mexico.

The geographical location of the company in the trade sector of the south central region of Mexico.

5.5.3 ANALYSIS OF THE SIZE OF THE FAMILY BUSINESS IN THE TRADE SECTOR AS A DETERMINING FACTOR IN ITS DEGREE OF COMPETITIVENESS

The INEGI classifies companies by size according to the number of workers and their annual sales. Micro enterprises in the trade sector include companies that have up to 10 workers with sales of up to 4 million pesos per year. Small companies have 11 to 30 workers and sales of 4.01 to 100 million pesos per year, and medium-sized companies have 31 to 100 workers and sales from 100.01 to 250 million pesos per year.

To carry out our analysis of the size of family businesses in the trade sector as a determining factor in the degree of competitiveness, in the survey we applied to entrepreneurs in the trade sector of the south central region of Mexico we asked them to state the number of workers in their companies.

Of the 165 companies surveyed, 52% were classified according to the INEGI as micro companies, since they had 1 to 10 workers.

Likewise, 35% of the companies surveyed are classified as small companies with 11 to 30 workers, only 10% of the companies surveyed are medium-sized, and 3% of the companies surveyed are large, with more than 101 workers.

The states in the South Central region of Mexico are primarily home to micro companies which have 1 to 10 workers. The state of Michoacán has 38 micro-businesses, followed by Puebla with 15, Querétaro with 12, 9 companies in Hidalgo, 8 micro companies in Tlaxcala, three in Guerrero and just one in Morelos.

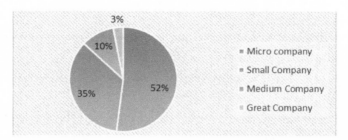

Fig. 9. Representation of the companies surveyed
according to INEGI classifications.

As can be seen in Fig. 9, of the companies surveyed, 52% are micro companies, 35% are small, 10% are medium-sized businesses and only 3% of the companies surveyed are large.

The companies in the south central region of Mexico that showed the highest percentage increase in level of competitiveness are those located in the states of Puebla, Querétaro and Hidalgo, with percentage increases of 23%, 20% and 21%, respectively. We also observed that in the state of Puebla there are 15 microenterprises, 12 in Querétaro and 9 in Hidalgo, so we can conclude that the size of the family business in the trade sector is a determining factor in its degree of competitiveness.

5.5.4 COMPETITIVENESS OF FAMILY BUSINESSES IN THE SOUTH CENTRAL REGION OF MEXICO DEPENDING ON THE STATE WHERE THEY ARE LOCATED

Likewise, as part of our study, we evaluated how the states companies are located in affects their competitiveness, where support programs in entrepreneurship training were located as well as financing programs in states in south central Mexico. This information was collected from the different chambers of commerce and economic development departments in the seven states of the region. The results are shown in Table 10.

Table 11. List of states of the South Central Region of Mexico that provide support for companies

State	Number of companies surveyed by state	% of companies by state	Training support program for companies	Business financing support program
Michoacán	74	45%	No	Yes
Puebla	30	18%	Yes	Yes
Querétaro	23	14%	Yes	Yes
Tlaxcala	15	9%	No	No
Hidalgo	15	9%	Yes	Yes

Guerrero	5	3%	No	No
Morelos	3	2%	No	No
Totals	165	100%		

In Table 11, we can see that the states that support training for businesses and support programs to finance them are Puebla, Queretaro and Hidalgo. This matches their increases in competitiveness.

5.6 CONCLUSIONS

Regarding the objective of testing whether the size of the company in the trade sector is a determining factor in its degree of competitiveness, we concluded that the size of the company in the trade sector is a determining factor in its degree of competitiveness, since 52% of the surveyed companies are micro companies, 35% are small companies, 10% are medium sized companies and only 3% of the companies surveyed are large. The companies in the south central region of Mexico that showed the highest percentage increase in level of competitiveness are those located in the states of Puebla, Querétaro and Hidalgo with a percentage increase of 23%, 20% and 21% respectively. The state of Puebla has 15 small businesses, there are 12 in the state of Querétaro and nine small businesses are located in the state of Hidalgo.

Regarding the objective of proving whether the location in a certain state affects the competitiveness of companies, our research allows us to conclude that, according to the results obtained, the states in which companies in the trade sector are located have an impact on their competitiveness. This can be affirmed on the basis of the information provided by Chambers of Commerce and economic development departments. The states of Puebla, Queretaro and Hidalgo have support programs for entrepreneurs, and these same states and Michoacán have financing programs for companies in the trade sector. We concluded that companies' location affects their competitiveness. Companies located in Puebla, Querétaro and Hidalgo are more competitive because of the access they have to financing and training programs provided by government institutions.

Regarding the general objective of testing whether the implementation of financing projects improves competitiveness of companies in the trade sector of the South Central Region of Mexico, including the states of Guerrero, Hidalgo, Michoacán, Morelos, Querétaro, Tlaxcala and Puebla, based on the results obtained in the survey and the analysis we performed, we concluded that the implementation of financing projects improves the competitiveness of companies in the trade sector of the South Central Region of Mexico.

5.7 FUTURE RESEARCH

In terms of future recommendations, the analysis presented here can be considered as a basis for the development of strategic planning analysis, enriched with proposals from companies in the trade sector or others. We also recommend that micro-, small and medium-sized businesses in the trade sector meet and generate analysis enriched with their experience and knowledge. Each company will be able to select and adapt the analysis of strategic planning to its characteristics, according to its needs, but in the end the general analysis will contain the essence of the analyses proposed by all the companies involved.

5.8 REFERENCES

Aguilar, JLE, Ayala, DGP, Martínez, RM and Méndez, ADG (2009). Strategic and competitive management of Mexican tourism companies : an empirical study. Magazine EAN, (66), 5-30.
Carrión, L., Zula, J., and Castillo, L. (2016). Analysis of management in small and medium enterprises and its application in the Catering industry in Ecuador. Administrative Science, (1), 82-102.

Domínguez, MJM (2014). Economic development, emerging countries and globalization. EXtoikos Magazine N. 14, pp. 5-14.

Goyzueta, RSI (2013). Management analysis for companies with growth and sustainability perspectives. Perspectives, Year 16 - N ° 31 - April 2013. pp. 87-132. Bolivian Catholic University San Pablo. Cochabamba

Hernández, AJC, Marín, GS, Del Valle, ID, and Castillo, M. Á. S. (2015). Competitive cultural orientations in the company / Competitive cultural orientation in the family business. Cuadernos de Estudios Empresariales, 25-49.

INEGI Economic Censuses (2018). Micro, small, medium and large company: stratification of establishments: Economic Censuses 2018 / National Institute of Statistics and Geography. Mexico: INEGI

Martínez, J. and Álvarez, C. (2006). Competitiveness map for the diagnosis of SMEs. In the memories XI Research Forum. International Congress of Accounting, Administration and Information Technology. Mexico DF

Muñoz, FJ, Salgado, RM and Rogela, JA (2014) Climate as a determining factor in shaping the company. Business Magazine.

OECD (2014) Perspectives on Global Development 2014: Boosting productivity to meet the middle-income challenge.

Pérez, MAI and Gilbert, SV (2015) Continuity in the company case analysis, Research Journal Edited by the Innovation and Development Area, SC

Pukall, TJ, and Calabró, A. (2013). The internationalization of family firms: A critical review and integrative model. Family Business Review, 27 (2), 103-125.

Romero, LE (2013). Competitiveness and productivity in SMEs An approach from family-company interaction. Magazine EAN, (57), 131-142.

Salgado, VHJ (2016). Companies facing the implementation of Management Control Systems. In Business Forum (Vol. 7, No. 2, pp. 56-81).

Saavedra, GML (2012). A proposal for the determination of competitiveness in the Latin American SME Pensamiento y Gestión, núm. 33, July-December, 2012, pp. 93-124 Universidad del Norte Barranquilla, Colombia.

SIEM (2018). Mexican Business Information System. Matrix of composition of companies and representativeness of the South Central Region of Mexico. https://siem.gob.mx/consulta.

Valenzuela, MM (2016). The competitiveness of the companies of the Valley of Mexicali Research Area: Environment of the organizations School of Engineering and Business, Autonomous University of Baja California Mexico.

Ward, J. (2006). Success in business. Bogotá: Editorial Norma.

World Economic Forum (2010). Global competitiveness report. Accessed April 12, 2017 http://www3.weforum.org/docs/WEF_GlobalCompetitivenessReport_2010-11.pdf

The Application of Information Technology to Special Needs Children: The Impact of Learning Media Objects on Mentally Disabled Children And Youth at C.A.M. No. 4

Sonia López Rodríguez, Margarita Lima Esteban, José Arcángel Zamora García, Eloina Herrera Rodríguez

Abstract Inclusive education has recently been expanding, making equal opportunities for all possible. The United Nations Educational, Scientific and Cultural Organization (UNESCO) has fought tirelessly against exclusion and inequalities in education. In Mexico, the Directorate General of Special Education (known in Spanish as Dirección General de Educación Especial) was created at the end of the 1970s, and Multi-Educational Centers (C.A.M. from the Spanish acronym for Centros de Atención Múltiples) first opened in 1990, with the reorganization and transformation of school-based services into special education programs. A CAM is an "educational institution that offers basic education to students with special education needs, with or without disabilities" (SEP, 2002). It also works with children on early intervention, pre-school, primary and workplace skills. The students are taught by specialized teachers. During the teaching and learning process, the children and youth at CAM No. 4 in Huamantla, Tlaxcala have little or no interaction with computers, a fundamental modern work tool. Accordingly, this study promotes the design and development of learning media objects to allow special needs children and youth to interact and find a place in society in order to participate in the Mexican economy and encourage their learning development.

Keywords Information technology, Learning object, Disability, Special needs children.

6.1 INTRODUCTION

At all educational levels, teaching-learning processes include the use of information technology, enabling teachers to create teaching-learning strategies adapted to disabled children and youth who have had very little interaction with computers. This is why this work describes the impact and performance of learning media objects specially designed and developed for these children and youth.

In the Convention of the Rights of Persons with Disabilities of 2017, in its preamble, Article 1, Subparagraph 2, "People with disabilities include those who have long-term physical, mental, intellectual or sensory impairments which in interaction with various barriers may hinder their full and effective participation in society on an equal basis with others."

This project is based on classifications by the National Institute of Statistics and Geography (in Spanish, Instituto Nacional de Estadística y Geografía, INEGI) which describes Group 1: Sensory and communication disabilities; Subgroup 131: communication and language comprehension disabilities; Group 2: motor disabilities; Subgroup 210: disabilities of the lower extremities, trunk, neck and head; Group 3: mental disabilities; Subgroup 310: intellectual disabilities, and Subgroup 320: behavioral and other mental disabilities.

The education sector needs to use information technology as a learning strategy so that disabled children and youth may enjoy and use these technological tools. A vital element for this study is the playfulness applied in developing learning media objects based on two teaching methods. First, the Montessori Method promotes an approach to reality in which each element is there for a reason in the environment of disabled children and youth. Next, the Decroly Method, based on children's basic needs, uses multimedia to support and maintain attention so that disabled children and youth may learn more.

Our study was carried out in collaboration with the staff at CAM No. 4 in Huamantla, Tlaxcala. At the CAM, we implemented learning media objects, measuring their impact and development over time.

6.2 CONCEPTUAL FRAMEWORK

6. 2. 1 HISTORICAL BACKGROUND OF DISABILITIES

Before the concept of persons with special needs, it was believed that they were socially, culturally and morally worthless. Therefore, people with disabilities remained isolated from society, making them victims of marginalization, discrimination, dependence and disrespect.

In the transition from the Middle Ages to the Renaissance, the acquisition of new knowledge and techniques increased curiosity for learning and stimulated human development and personality training (Hernández, 2001).

In the 17th and 18th centuries, the mentally disabled were placed in orphanages, asylums, prisons and other government institutions. There they were locked up with criminals and the elderly.

In the late 18th century and early 19th century, the period of the specialized institutionalization of disabled persons began with the emergence of special education.

Starting in the 1960s and especially in the 1970s, a profound change occurred in the conception of deficiency and special education, and three highly relevant aspects generated societal change in the way people with disabilities were perceived: 1) development and deficiency disorders were identified, 2) a new perspective emphasized learning processes and difficulties encountered by students during their progress, and 3) evaluation methods focused on learning processes and necessary aid according to the deficiency category (Mina, 2005).

In the early 20th century, special education got a boost from the Montessori Method in Italy and the Decroly Method in Belgium. Educational methods subsequently identified that achieving efficiency should be based on the progressive development of each student according to their physical, mental, social and academic needs, responding to the community's demands. All programs and educational systems are based on the relationship between learning styles and intelligence (María Celeste Gatto, 2005).

Starting in 1993, as a result of the National Agreement for the Modernization of Basic Education (known in Spanish as Acuerdo Nacional para la Modernización de la Educación Básica) - an amendment to Art. 27 of the Mexican Constitution and the enactment of the General Education Law - a substantial reorientation and reorganization of special education services was implemented (SEP, 2002).

As a consequence of changes in special education, its reorganization was promoted and an educational guide according to the special education needs of students was incorporated into the basic education syllabus, leading to a new reorganization as follows:

- Transformation of special education school-based services into CAMs, defined as "educational institutions that offer basic education for students with special educational needs, with or without disabilities." CAMs offer different levels of basic education using adapted school curricula and general study programs. Groups are also organized in terms of pupils' ages, placing students with disabilities in a single group.
- Establishment of Support Service Units for Regular Education (known in Spanish as Unidades de Servicios de Apoyo a la Educación Regular, USAER) to promote the inclusion of children with disabilities in early education classes and regular basic education. These units were formed mainly with existing staff. The preservation of Preschool Psychopedagogical Care Centers (known in Spanish as Centros de Atención Psicopedagógica de Educación Preescolar, CAPEP) was also encouraged in support services for kindergartens.
- Creation of Public Orientation Units (known in Spanish as Unidades de Orientación Pública, U.O.P.) to provide information and specialized instruction to parents and teachers (SEP, 2002).
- One of the major achievements recorded in the disability sector in Mexico occurred on May 30, 2011 during the government of Mexican President Felipe Calderon, when the General Law for the Inclusion of Persons with Disabilities was approved. Its objective is:

"Regulate Art. 1 of the Mexican Constitution by setting the conditions by which the State promotes and protects the unfettered exercise of human rights and fundamental freedoms of persons with disabilities, ensuring their full inclusion in society with respect, equality and equal opportunities." (Ley General para la Inclusión de las Personas con Discapacidad, 2011).

Chapter 3 of the General Law for the Inclusion of People with Disabilities, Art. 12, Paragraph II, supports:

"Promoting the inclusion of people with disabilities at all levels of the National Education System by developing and applying rules and regulations in order to avoid their discrimination, accessibility requirements in school facilities and teaching materials and technical support will be provided, with trained educational personnel".

Fraction VI calls for:

"Giving students with disabilities materials and technical needs that support their academic performance by equipping schools and teaching centers with Braille books, learning materials, Mexican sign language interpreters or Braille specialists, computerized equipment with technology for the blind and all supports identified as necessary to provide quality education". (Ley General para la Inclusión de las Personas con Discapacidad, 2011).

6. 2. 2 DISABILITY CONCEPT AND TYPES ACCORDING TO THE GENERAL LAW FOR THE INCLUSION OF PERSONS WITH DISABILITIES IN MEXICO

In the General Law for the Inclusion of Persons with Disabilities, Art. 2, an addendum to Section DOF 22-06-2018 (DOF: Diario Oficial de la Federación - Official Federal Gazette) states:

IX. "Disability. It is the consequence of the disability or limitation of a person who when he or she interacts with the barriers imposed by a social environment, may hinder their full, effective participation in society on an equal basis with others.

The following sections describe the types of disability recognized by law:

X. Physical disability. It is a sequel or malformation as a result of a disorder of the peripheral neuromuscular system, causing an alteration in control over movement and posture. It may hinder their full effective participation in society on an equal basis with others. Addendum DOF 22-06-2018.

XI. Mental disability. Abnormalities or deficiencies in the neuronal system of a person, which, combined with a series of events that he or she cannot control, trigger a change in behavior and impede his or her development and social coexistence, and when interacting with the barriers imposed by a social environment, may hinder his or her full effective participation in society on an equal basis with others. Addendum DOF 22-06-2018.

XII. Intellectual disability. It is characterized by significant limitations both in the structure of reasoned thinking and in the adaptive behavior of the person, and when interacting with the barriers imposed by a social environment, it may hinder their full effective participation in society on an equal basis with others.

XII. Sensory impairment. It is the structural or functional impairment of sight, hearing, taste, smell or touch, as well as the structures and functions associated with each one, and when interacting with the barriers imposed by a social environment, it may hinder their full effective participation in society on an equal basis with others. Addendum DOF 22-06-2018 (Ley General para la Inclusión de las Personas con Discapacidad, 2011).

Considering that these types of disabilities are included in the five proposed groups by the National Institute of Statistics and Geography in 2001, we will use this classifier, which is specifically described in the methodology.

6.2.3 Method applied to special education teaching

6.2.3.1 Montessori Method

In the 19th century, special education began to develop in Europe. In this century, authors such as Pinel (1745-1826), Esquirol (1772-1840), Itard (1774-1836) and Seguin (1812-1880) developed methods applied to disabilities which were improved upon by Ovide Decroly and Maria Montessori in the 20th century.

In 1918, Maria Montessori published a book entitled Advanced Methodology, which contributed to special education (Espejo, 2009).

The Montessori Method helps children reach their potential as human beings through their senses in a dedicated environment, through the scientific observation of a well-trained teacher. In this method "The educational goal should be to cultivate the natural desire to learn", so many grades make up each group, ensuring age diversity.

Older children help younger children, who in turn remind them of forgotten concepts. In the method, children move at their own pace through tasks set by the teacher in the classroom, freeing them to develop by themselves in a structured environment. The material used in this method helps children understand what they learn by associating abstract concepts with concrete sensory experience in order to learn, not just memorize.

The method is based on sensorial education and uses the five senses: sight, taste, touch, smell and hearing. The aim of the exercises is to educate the senses so children learn about the environment and are able to discriminate its subtlest aspects (Discapacidad, 2016).

The Montessori Method is considered education for life, and it has the following characteristics:

- It aids human natural development.
- The child is stimulated to form his/her own character and express his/her own personality, gaining security and respect.
- It aims to support the responsibility and development of self-discipline, helping children become independent and free.
- The child is guided in his/her spiritual and intellectual training.

6. 2. 3. 2 The Decroly Method

This teaching method is based on intuitive, concrete, experimental and reasoned sensations associated with direct observation and expression in all its forms. This way, only abstract concepts reach the child, almost imperceptibly. At the New Education Congress held in Calanis in 1921, the specific characteristics of schools founded according to this method were set:

1. The school must operate in a natural environment for 15 years. In other words, the school must be in an environment where the child can observe natural phenomena, the life of living beings, especially human beings, and adapt to existing conditions.

2. The school should have a small number of children of both sexes and all ages – from four to 15 years old.

3. The workshop-classrooms are to be furnished and equipped in such a way that they may become small laboratories.

4. Staff will be active, intelligent, creative, prepared to observe plants, animals and children, and will love children. They must also be open to receiving training in psychology and science; they must express themselves well and have a sense of order and discipline.

5. Schools must group children with as much homogeneity as possible, with no more than 25 children.

6. For children who are irregular or lagging behind, groups will be from 10 to 15. Teachers must prepare special classes in which work will be led by an expert, helping children who are lagging to progress by stimulating the capacities of different students.

7. Language and calculus classes will be given preferably in the morning at least three or four times a week during the first hour of class, with exercises through games in which success will be the main motivator.

8. The beginning of the morning session will not involve technical classes, but rather different exercises such as observation, comparison, association, crafts, art, singing and physical games.

9. The afternoons will focus on crafts and languages.

10. Some mornings will be used for excursions and visits (aquatic animals and fishing, insect hunting, factory visits, museums, stations, craft workshops).
11. Parents will be made aware of the method used in the school in order to understand it and assist in its effectiveness.
12. The school will help children understand what they do and persuade them to discipline themselves.
13. It will develop initiative and self-confidence. Children will give lectures to their classmates.

Psychophysiological basis:

In 1901, Decroly created a school for so-called 'normal children' and in 1907 the 'for life and through life' school. He followed children's study day by day, considering the following:

1. The syllabus of a school whose goal is learning for life must be based on the needs of women and men according to their psychological and social conditions, such as eating, sleeping, shelter, defending themselves against risks, psychic development and vocational training.
2. Teachers must ensure that children develop the habit and taste for work and study, making lessons attractive by constantly stimulating children's senses.
3. Teachers talk very little in this method. The approach is a few words and many facts: presenting, doing, observing, analyzing, manipulating, building and collecting.
4. Teachers will endeavor to provide children with full satisfaction of their activity and movement needs, because muscle memory is an indisputably powerful resource to ensure the durability of knowledge.
5. The school is everywhere. The kitchen, dining room, garden, field, farm, workshop, factory, quarry, warehouses, museums, exhibitions, excursions and trips provide more learning than classroom work.

6. Education aims to provide children with good methodology. Children are taught to use library books and request information and/or orientation.
7. The aim of language and speech exercises is to provide vocabulary connected to concrete reality to the child.
8. Children will be able to graduate and progress, remembering information about ages, food, clothes, housing, furniture, weapons, trade, industry, tools, culture, administration and customs.

School, according to Decroly, prepares children for social life and it must give them knowledge about their own personality: consciousness of 'I', needs, goals and aspirations. Children must be aware of the natural environment in which they live and on which they depend in order to reach their goals.

6. 2. 4 Media learning objects

6.2.4.1 Concept

The term 'Learning Object' was first coined in 1992 by Wayne, who associated the Lego® brick with standardized learning bricks for reutilization purposes in educational processes (Hodgins, 2000).

The concept is quite broad, but Jose Valdeni and other authors in the work "Multimodal Learning Objects" advanced the idea that these bricks are educational contents which may be reutilized in different training cycles, as well as virtual learning environments and platforms that contribute to the cost reduction of materials production. They also observed planned segments used in institutions in order to reuse them, and they mention a type of design in non-sequential independent modules in which each object can be used individually with other resources in different contexts, responding to different needs and learning styles. (José Valdeni de Lima, 2014).

Our aim is to contrast the concept of the learning object and focus it on education. A Colombian magazine article defines it as a virtual object and pedagogical mediator, intentionally designed for a learning purpose and useful in various educational contexts. (Callejas Cuervo, Hernández Niño & Pinzón Villamil, 2011).

6.2.4.2 Characteristics

- Reusability in different contexts.
- Modularity, block-building.
- Multiplatform portability.
- Metadata, ID tags of contents.

It is important and necessary that the learning object not be limited to a single education or training context. The media learning objects we studied may also be used by children without disabilities from two to five years' old who are starting their interaction with computers in order to promote the knowledge and identification of their immediate environment and their basic physiological needs.

6. 2. 5 Influence of games on special needs children

In 1959, the United Nations General Assembly, and in 1990, the Spanish Parliament, ratified that play is a right for children and we, as adults, must ensure their rights are respected. Children with disabilities have the right to play and access toys, but some have serious difficulties when using some games and toys on the market.

Games enable them to develop their physical and mental abilities. Games are a source of self-affirmation, satisfaction and pleasure. Playing helps to be active and prepare for adult life. Insufficient play during childhood causes incomplete personality development in children.

Types of disabilities assessed:

Visual impairment: Children with visual problems have been included to assess toys, both those who have some sight remaining and those who are completely blind.

Hearing impairment: Children with hearing problems have been included to assess toys, both those who have some hearing remaining and those who are completely deaf.

Motor impairment: Children with important carriage and manipulation problems have been included to assess toys.

Toy typologies (ESAR system)

Exercise games: They consist of repeating an action over and over for the pleasure of immediate results.

Symbolic games: They involve the representation of an object by another.

Role-playing games imitating adults for children include:

Assembly games: These involve pieces to fit, assemble, overlap, stack or join.

Rule games: These include a set of directions or rules players should know and respect.

Toys for children with visual impairments must:

- Have a simple, realistic design, easy to identify by touch.
- Include easy to manipulate accessories.
- Incorporate sound effects and different textures.
- Not have many small pieces.
- Have bright, contrasting colors to be perceived by children with sight remaining.
- Have compact pieces that are not disassembled easily.

Adapted toys for people who are blind or visually impaired:

Chess: The white squares of the chess board for the blind are below the black squares so the player knows whether the square is white or black. There is also a small hole in the center of each square to pin the pieces. The black chess pieces have protruding pins on the head to distinguish them from the white chess pieces. Both the black and white chess pieces have a downward pin which is inserted into the hole on the board to keep them secure and affixed during the game.

Giant Spanish playing card decks: The giant print playing cards are larger than an average pack. (12.5 x 19 cm.).

Adapted bingo cards: Each box has raised numbers with corresponding Braille below them. Where there is no number, the texture is different.

Raised Parcheesi uses the same technique as for chess. The pieces are not flat, but each color has a different shape for identification (Costa et. al, 2007).

6. 2. 6 CAM No. 4, Tlaxcala

In accordance with the standards established in Article 3 of the Mexican Constitution, "Every individual is entitled to receive an education. The government - federal, states, capital and municipalities - shall provide pre-school, elementary, secondary and high school education, which together make up basic education in Mexico. Middle and high school education shall be compulsory." (Mexican Constitution (Constitución Política de los Estados Unidos Mexicanos).

According to Agreement 592 and the 2011 curriculum, education is a fundamental right and a strategy for expanding opportunities, implementing intercultural relations, reducing inequalities between social groups, closing gaps and fostering equality.

The educational system recognizes the cultural diversity that exists in Mexico, and makes the right to education effective by providing inclusive, relevant education (Irazabal, 2011).

Art. 4 states that "disabled persons shall enjoy the same rights recognized by the Mexican legal system, regardless of ethnicity, nationality, gender, age, level of disability, socioeconomic status, health condition, religion, opinions, marital status, sexual preference, pregnancy, political identity, language, immigration status or any other reason or characteristic. Anti-discrimination measures are aimed at preventing or correcting the fact that a person with a disability may be treated less favorably than another person in a similar situation." (Diario Oficial de la Federación, 2011).

The educational sector program develops new forms and educational service locations for the inclusion of people with disabilities and exceptional abilities at all educational levels by:

- Providing administrative and teaching personnel with technical and educational support to facilitate the full inclusion of disabled students.
- Adapting and equipping all educational establishments in order to remove physical barriers that reduce the access and participation of disabled students (SEP, 2013).

In the state of Tlaxcala, there are nineteen CAMs in different municipalities. All of them have managed to remain open. Nevertheless, there are gaps in educational opportunities that require particular attention.

CAMs, including CAM No. 4 in Huamantla, provide pre-school and elementary educational and vocational training for disabled youth 15 to 22 years old (Educativa, 2013). CAMs tend to students regular schools have not integrated by providing them with relevant education and specific assistance in order to allow them to participate fully and continue learning.

CAM No. 4 Huamantla is currently directed by L.E.E. Alicia López Anaya, who along with her teaching staff provides initial education and training skills along with psychological and technical support. CAM No. 4 Huamantla has an elementary school teacher, a workshop instructor and a job training instructor. The technical support team includes a psychologist, social worker, language teacher, support teacher, physical therapist and physical education teacher. Currently, all of them tend to 54 students in pre-school and primary school with special needs such as motor skills, hearing and autism, among others.

6.3 THE DEVELOPMENT PROCESS OF MEDIA LEARNING OBJECTS

In 2016, from May to August, we had our first meeting at the CAM in Santa Ana Xalmimilulco, Huejotzingo, Puebla. We performed an information technology needs survey. All the teachers who were in direct contact with children were involved in the study.

6. 3. 1. SPECIFICATIONS

A summary was written with the main requirements which were the result of six observation cycles, validated by expert special education teachers who interact with special needs children and youth. The requirements are the following:

Learning objects for farm animals.

Functional requirements:

- Placement of children and youth in four contexts in order to identify stable, farm, house and pasture animals.
- Generation of distinct environments for each area of animals (outdoors, close to home, at home).

Design and multimedia requirements:

- Interface moving objects to draw attention.
- Realistic sounds.
- Narrator with a voice and interaction with the user.
- Sound of the selected animal, interaction with the user, no limit to reproductions.
- True colors of each animal.
- Bright colors to capture the attention of children and youth.

Learning objects for basic needs and feelings.

Functional requirements:

- Real-life environments.
- Showing the specific elements of each feeling.
- Animated simulation on the process of urinating, flushing toilets and washing hands.
- Animated simulation on brushing teeth.

Design and multimedia requirements:

- Dynamic display pictures that change with mood: happy, ill, angry, sad and scared. Audio interaction with the user.
- Blue background for comfort of navigation.
- Bright colors to capture the attention of children and youth.
- Large letters and white text to describe the activities as the simulation progresses.

Learning objects for healthy food.

Functional requirements:

- Junk and healthy food identification. Voice interaction: What would you like to eat?
- Principal fruits and vegetables on Clipart, inspiring confidence and happiness.
- Junk and healthy food on Clipart.

Design and multimedia requirements:

- Sound of the name of the fruit or vegetable in each interaction with the user, no limit to reproductions.
- Real sounds.
- Blue background for comfort of navigation.
- Bright colors to capture the attention of children and youth.

- Large letters and white text to describe the activities as the simulation progresses.
- Large images, preferably a girl or a boy.

Learning objects for uppercase and lowercase alphabet.

Functional requirements:

- Alphabet stroke simulation in uppercase.
- Alphabetic stroke simulation in lowercase.
- Slow, steady strokes.

Design and multimedia requirements:

- Each letter must contain its corresponding audio description.
- Each letter must refer to a word as an example. Then, each stroke must be slow.
- Bright colors to capture the attention of children and youth.
- Large letters.

Learning objects for the ecosystem.

Functional requirements:

- Simulation of animals from aquatic ecosystems, specifically, the marine ecosystem.
- Simulation of animals from land ecosystems: forest, tundra, desert and jungle.
- Simulation of the activities of each animal. Real sounds.
- Distinctive environments within the ecosystem.

Design and multimedia requirements:

- Bright colors to capture the attention of children and youth.
- Large pictures.

For this study, the creative ideas of students over five four-month periods were integrated through teachers' careful planning and instructions. Students implemented their knowledge on Multimedia I and Multimedia II for the learning objects, using Montessori and Decroly pedagogical approaches.

6. 3. 2 Development methodology

In accordance with the nature of the project, an incremental or prototype model was applied, which followed flexible, changing requirements through an experimental cycle. Initially, we used this method because we sought to satisfy a set of requirements from a stable base, and the missing requirements evolved from phase to phase (Areba, 2001). Since the requirements were often fulfilled, we obtained different versions of the final product until the group of experts approved them and the CAM in Santa Ana Xalmimilulco, Huejotzingo, Puebla implemented them. CAM No. 4 in Huamantla is currently using these media learning objects.

6. 3. 2. 1 First approach of the description

The initial requirements were set forth in
the development of the project:

The media learning objects were designed to work locally on the computers of CAM No. 4 in Huamantla. These objects allow disabled children and youth to identify domestic and farm animals and learn the alphabet with its corresponding keystrokes in upper and lower cases. This media learning project also allows children to interact with ecosystems and show their basic physiological needs.

After general needs had been identified, students did brainstorming. Next, the first prototype of each learning project was constituted. They were unrealistic because they were oriented towards intellectually competent children, with short pauses, quick strokes and dull colors. Then, requirements analysis began and the samples were oriented towards special needs children and youth. The sounds were defined to avoid scaring users. The colors and shapes were also chosen. In addition, each version was focused on the Montessori and Decroly learning methods.

6. 3. 2. 2 Development

This project emerged from a concept or pre-production: a preliminary design was developed. Then, designing the characters was suggested using Adobe Illustrator® tools. We also tested a combination of characters which seemed harmless and attractive, creating a high level of identification and confidence for users.

By editing different pictures, Adobe Photoshop® tools were used to prepare landscapes and surroundings which allowed characters to be located in a realistic environment. This allowed users to enjoy an enriching experience with the sounds of each animal through experiential interaction.

For the learning object to offer interaction through use of a mouse, different events were programmed with Adobe Animate® tools in order to enable Human-Computer interaction.

Finally, sounds showed satisfactory progress. Student voices were tested, resulting in a less than ideal tone for the learning objects. Next, we tried children's voices, which sounded like they were from a cartoon, encouraging greater confidence and the acceptance of learning objects by disabled children and youth.

For audio editing, we used Adobe Audition®. The voice was recorded and edited to find the ideal tone for each objective of the different learning objects.

6. 3. 2. 3 Pedagogical approach

The teacher's primary work is to use techniques and strategies that allow him or her to achieve the highest impact on the student's metacognition. This study seeks to generate educational software based on learning activities and the contextualization of elements through the incorporation of information and communication technologies.

Alvaro H. Galvis Panqueva, in 'Educational Software Engineering', coins the term MEC and mentions educational software, referring to it as computer applications whose end goal is to support learning.

In the same work, categories of MEC are identified: algorithmic, oriented to transmit something, and heuristic, oriented to build knowledge on an object of study (Galvis, 1997). This work refers to the design and construction of software based on heuristic classification, in which specific educational needs are identified to guide construction of knowledge on a particular object, constituting educational materials through the computer to generate reusable learning objects that allow special needs children and youth to benefit from a teaching-learning environment.

Besides examining the pedagogical aspects to be considered in constructing learning objects, from the Montessori teaching method we drew the idea of stimulating a specific sensory experience by promoting adapted environments for learning, generating didactic material as tools to help understand what is learned. It has been established that a human being must be formed through the senses and cultivated through the motivation of the natural desire to learn. This is why realistic environments are included in the learning objects, real sounds and interaction with the user, to make it possible to acquire knowledge through interaction, motivation and senses, promoting freedom and independence.

In accordance with the Decroly method, oriented towards special education, materials are produced considering the environment in which the child develops based on experimental sensation, promoting observation and contact with the environment (plants, animals and people), referring to natural phenomena and beings in general, promoting exercises such as stimulation games and the pleasure of success. Interaction with learning objects is based on stimulation and play through scenarios in which special needs children and youth can relate their previously acquired knowledge to new knowledge.

6.4 FINAL VERSION

The final result emerged once the evaluation and validation process had been carried out by experts after six cycles of the incremental or evolutionary model. It is described below.

"Getting to know pets and farm animals" multimedia learning object

This learning object has cartoon-like animation in which characters have repetitive movements. Interaction is done through a rooster avatar which accompanies children during their tour of the farm.

To give life to the farm we had to create characters, strokes and colors; background environments were achieved by creating and editing different images in order to give an appearance of comfort and ensure interaction with the user. This followed the approach of achieving learning experience through stimulus and response, allowing interaction at all times between the learning object and user.

"Getting to know ecosystems" multimedia learning object

This learning object allows children to get to know the different ecosystems and animals that inhabit marine and land ecosystems. Different styles of images were combined to highlight the different ecosystems, allowing for a more realistic, enriching user experience. The sounds of various characters were edited to obtain real animal sounds, and for wild animals the bass of the audio track was reinforced.

"Alphabet" multimedia learning object

This learning object exemplifies the stroke to type each letter of the Mexican alphabet in upper and lower case. The object is composed of a letter-tracing simulation as well as a child's voice indicating the full name of the letter and the word that refers to it.

The color specifications that enhance the stroke were considered as a whole. We emphasized the need to use a background simulating a notebook to bring children and youth closer to a real context, as well as the red color of the stroke.

Navigation is done through a menu in which children can choose the letter for which the stroke will be made, with repeating forward and back buttons. This improves the user experience: each example has a reproduction sound, an image and a letter of the alphabet.

"Basic Needs" multimedia learning object

This learning object contains several submodules developed according to requirements in order to access each menu, where users can choose options such as emotions, healthy food and useful activities. A back button enables users to explore the entire learning object, and they may navigate through all the options as many times as necessary.

6. 5 IMPLEMENTATION

Once development was completed and the specifications and validation cycles of the incremental model had been covered, authorization was requested to implement the learning objectives at the CAM in Santa Ana Xalmimilulco, Huejotzingo, Puebla. The first phase of implementation and first application of the observation guide were carried out, identifying the reactions, behaviors and stimuli of special needs children and youth in October 2016. Later, we learned that there was a CAM No. 4 in Huamantla, Tlaxcala, where the learning objects were presented and underwent minimal modifications by experts after meetings in early 2017. Implementation and start-up took a year because CAM No. 4 did not have computer equipment for the installation and implementation of learning objects.

It was not until July 17; 2018 that formal implementation of the learning objects was carried out. The second observation guide was created, documenting the reactions, behaviors and stimuli observed when the objects were used.

6.6 QUALITATIVE ANALYSIS OF THE IMPACT OF LEARNING OBJECTS

6.6.1 REFLECTIONS AND PRIOR ORGANIZATION

After ten months of implementation and continuous use of learning objects, the impact on the teaching of special needs children and youth can be measured over time and with historical data from two observation guide applications, yielding similar results from one group to another in both applications of the qualitative instrument.

To determine the scope of the study, the document from the National Institute of Statistics, Geography and Information (INEGI), called "Classification of Type of Disability - Historical", is used as a base for the categorization of deficiencies and disabilities according to the organ, function or area of the body affected, or where the limitation manifests itself (National Institute of Statistics, 2001).

Next, the classification of types of disabilities is described, which according to the INEGI document revised is organized into two levels: group and subgroup. The disability groups identified by a key are the following:

Group 1 Sensory and communication disabilities
Group 2 Motor disabilities
Group 3 Mental disabilities
Group 4 Multiple disabilities and others
Group 9 Special keys

Sensory and communication disabilities include impairments and disabilities of sight, hearing and speech, for example, blindness, loss of an eye, loss of sight in one eye, deafness, hearing loss on one side and muteness, among others.

The motor group includes deficiencies and disabilities to walk, manipulate objects and coordinate movements, as well as to use arms and hands. The mental group includes intellectual and behavioral deficiencies that cause restrictions on learning and behavior, so that the person cannot relate to the environment and has limitations in the performance of his or her activities. The group of multiple disabilities and others contains combinations of the restrictions described above, for example, mental retardation and muteness, blindness and deafness, among others.

The second level (subgroup), is identified by three digits, with the first one on the left. The group to which they belong is identified, and in all the classification includes 18 subgroups.

Each subgroup is made up of a list in alphabetical order of descriptions related to deficiencies and disabilities; it includes both technical names and synonyms by which people recognize disabilities. Thus, for the same deficiency or disability several descriptions may appear. In some cases, its synonym is placed in parentheses (National Institute of Statistics, 2001).

Although in general the specialists mentioned in the theoretical framework divide motor, sensory and mental disabilities in the classifier according to INEGI, no clinical or medical criteria were applied since the information that is classified consists of the descriptions people provided. The children selected as part of the research sample were determined by the teachers at the CAM because they know the deficiencies and disabilities of each child and which classification each child is in.

Table 12 identifies the disabilities of the beneficiaries of the proposed learning objects. As a result, a first classification is made of the children and youth.

Table 12. Range of disabilities for the proposed learning objects

Group	Disabilities	Description	Subgroup
Group 1	Sensory and communication disabilities	Disabilities to see, hear and speak.	Subgroup 110 disabilities to see. Subgroup 120 hearing disabilities. Subgroup 130 disabilities to speak (muteness). Subgroup 131 communication disabilities and language comprehension. Subgroup 199 insufficiently specified group of sensory disabilities and communication.
Group 2	Mobility disabilities	Disabilities to walk, manipulate objects and coordinate movements to carry out activities of daily life	Subgroup 210 disabilities of the lower extremities, trunk, neck and head Subgroup 220 disabilities of the upper extremities Subgroup 299 insufficiently specified from the motor disabilities group
Group 3	Mental disabilities	Disabilities to learn and behave, both in daily activities and relationship with other people	Subgroup 310 intellectual disabilities (mental retardation) Subgroup 320 behavioral and other mental disabilities Subgroup 399 insufficiently specified mental disability group
Group 4	Multiple disabilities and others	Multiple disabilities that do not correspond to groups 1, 2 and 3.	Subgroup 401-422 multiple disabilities Subgroup 430 other types of disabilities Subgroup 499 insufficiently specified group of multiple disabilities and other

Group 9	Special keys	Seeks to refine the descriptions collected in the field that do not correspond to the concept of disability	Subgroup 960 type of disability not specified Subgroup 970 descriptions that do not correspond to the concept of disability subgroup 980 does not know subgroup 999 unspecified general

6.6.2 Data collection

Data collection was done three times, initially on October 25, 2016 with a group of 18 children at the CAM in Santa Ana Xalmimilulco, Puebla, according to the classifier, which establishes that learning objects are aimed only at certain groups, including specifically highlighted subgroups. The learning objects include Group 1, "Sensory and communication disabilities", including Subgroup 131, communication disabilities and language comprehension; Group 2, called "Motor disabilities", specifically covering Subgroup 210 referring to disabilities of the lower extremities, trunk, neck and head, and finally, Group 3, "Mental disabilities", covering Subgroup 310, referring to intellectual disabilities (mental retardation) and Subgroup 320, behavioral and other mental disabilities (National Institute of Statistics, 2001).

Subsequently, on July 17, 2018 at CAM No. 4 in Huamantla, instrument version 2 was applied to 16 special needs children and youth. It included a brief qualitative interview consisting of two key questions on management and interactivity for disabled boys, girls and youth: What did you learn? Where will you apply what you learned? The conditions and characteristics of the second group allowed for this type of interaction. The two instruments were taken as a source of primary information and secondary information on performance was generated over time, collected through experiences and demonstrations regarding the performance that special needs children and youth displayed when using the learning objects, generated by the director of CAM No. 4, L.E.E. Alicia López Anaya, and her teaching and psycho-pedagogical support teams. The people involved in teaching processes, teachers and experts, through their experience in the use of learning objects, accompany special needs children and youth in their use.

6. 6. 3 ANALYSIS CATEGORIES

6. 6. 3. 1 Definition, description and coding of analysis categories

According to Miles and Huberman (1984), qualitative research is interested in everyday situations. In this report, one of three sub-processes is used to perform analysis, referring to the reduction of data, oriented towards its selection and condensation, through codification and the relation of topics, this is why we present our findings through conceptual models which are easy to understand for readers.

For the collection of information, an observation instrument is used in a natural context, applied twice with similar results, in order to achieve reliability.

Of a total of 54 disabled children and youth 34 tests were performed, representing 100% of Groups 1, 2 and 3 and the subgroups: 18 observation guides with version 1 of the instrument and 16 with version 2, including the completion of the proposed interview described above. Initially, three categories were considered with three subcategories each, as described below:

CGO-01 Concerning the description of performance, it was observed and recorded through supervised practices and activities.

Subcategories

CGO-O1.1. Conduct (how a person conducts him or herself in normal, moral, social and cultural relationships with others.)

CGO-O1.2. Behavior (ways to conduct oneself and react to a stimulus in relation to the environment).

CGO-O1.3. Attitudes (behavior of the special needs child or youth when handling the system).

CGO-02 Comparison of new knowledge with previous knowledge. This was observed and recorded through supervised practices and activities.

Subcategories

CGO-02.1. Visual impact, attracting attention

CGO-02.2. User friendliness, easy and proper handling, after observation of the use of the learning object by the applicator.

CGO-02.3. Feeling/stimulation, the desire to use the learning object through motivation by images and sounds.

CGO-03 Retention and transfer. The patterns found in the textual responses expressed by special needs children and youth are described in a qualitative micro-interview applied to 14 children whose condition allows them to communicate their feelings and perceptions.

6. 7 RESULTS

6. 7. 1 GENERATION OF THEORIES AND EXPLANATIONS

We noted that the learning object for healthy food was not significant for disabled children and youth because only 11.7% (4 of 34) children explored or studied it. The researchers associated this situation with the fact that disabled children and youth do not choose what they eat, since this is associated with each individual situation and with the medicine that is ingested. It is associated with the fact that disabled children and youth have not tried foods outside of their medical diet.

We found some interesting data. Since special needs children and youth refer to the sound of farm animals, this learning object had great acceptance because in their environment, their homes or near their homes they have seen similar animals. They perfectly associate things they know, which is why they feel identified and attracted to this learning object compared to other objects.

It was observed that of the children who were attracted to the learning object to type the alphabet in uppercase and lowercase, 78% of them try to simulate the stroke on the computer screen, and they are stimulated by the motivation of the associated word and the applause sound.

Comments from teachers and experts who have used learning objects over time (July 2018-May 2019) have also been taken into consideration:

- Children now approach the computer with confidence.
- Reinforcement of their cognitive processes has been observed in terms of memory, attention and thinking.
- Students' attention has improved through eye-catching, interactive material.
- Their motivation to learn has been strengthened.
- There has been a reinforcement of learning in Spanish, mathematics, knowledge of the natural and social environment and art.
- Communication has improved.
- There has been greater interaction with peers, strengthening socialization.
- Visual memory has been reinforced.
- The prediction and anticipation of events of a narration or event have been reinforced.
- Modeling of student behavior has been observed.

These comments were expressed by the experts at CAM No. 4 in Huamantla, Tlaxcala who interact with special needs children and youth, led by director L.E.E. Alicia López Anaya, in document 062/2018-2019 dated May 13, 2019, in which they answered the question: What positive impact do multimedia learning objects have on children over time?

It can clearly be observed that learning objects have been a watershed event in the academic performance of special needs children and youth. Through a motivational, playful approach, the knowledge, approach and use of computer equipment have been encouraged.

6.8 CONCLUSIONS

The promotion of fun activities that are attractive and motivating to special needs children provides a teaching tool for teachers who perform the important human task of sharing knowledge with their students.

With regards to performance, a positive, proactive attitude was observed in special needs children and youth, showing emotional transparency in reaction to stimuli. We observed great attention to visual and auditory stimuli; learning objects were used without browsing rules, as special needs children and youth navigate from side to side between objects according to their interest and listen repeatedly to the sounds and applause emitted in the learning objects. Physical and oral manifestations of emotion are noted during their achievements and interactions with the system. 1 in 10 children who used the learning objects remained seated and silent, but they were constantly attentive to the visual impact and the sounds.

In terms of identifying aspects of the relationship of new knowledge to prior knowledge, we observed and recorded that learning objects have a visual impact. Although a previous demonstration is made of how learning objects are browsed sequentially until the achievement of specific knowledge by the instrument's applicator, they do not have or impose browsing rules for special needs children. Since users browse without sequence being important, they seek interaction with learning objects that attract their attention and in which they find simulated environments similar to their own.

In terms of retention and transfer, after analysis of recorded data it was noted that some learning objects had a greater impact on special needs children and youth because the applicators observed that users spend more time on learning objects dealing with the farm and ecosystems, observing the shapes of the animals, their environments, and listening repeatedly to the sounds emitted by each animal. After interaction with the learning object, the user feels a need to move and address the object he or she wants to hear by using the mouse. Identification is found at the next level of the learning object: basic physiological needs, in which the child observes and listens to the process of going to the bathroom and washing the hands and teeth as part of the hygiene routine. Finally, on level three, attention is drawn to the learning object, which shows the slow stroke of the alphabet in uppercase and lowercase letters, encouraging users to attempt the stroke repeatedly and associate the stroke with a word, observing the application of learning and stimulating achievements through applause.

Special needs children and youth who are able to express their feelings and impressions about learning objects openly state that what they have learned will be useful in their school, home and family environments.

Exploring educational best practices using information technology encourages special needs users to approach computer-based tools, allowing them to identify computer use as a fun way of learning and obtaining life experience.

6.9 REFERENCES

Areba, J. B. (2001). Metodología del analisis estructurado de sistemas. Madrid España: Universidad Pontificia.

Callejas Cuervo, M., Hernández Niño, E. J., & Pinzón Villamil, J. N. (2011). Objetos de aprendizaje, un estado del arte. Entramado, 176-189.

Constitución politica de los Estados unidos Mexicanos. (s.f.). Obtenido de Artículo 3o. Todo individuo tiene derecho a recibir educación. El Estado –Federación, Estados, Distrito Federal y Municipios–, impartirá educación preescolar, http://www.diputados.gob.mx/LeyesBiblio/htm/1.htm

Costa, M., & ET.AL, R. (2007). Juegos. juguetes y discapacidad. Alicante, España.

Diario Oficial de la Federación. (30 de mayo de 2011). Ley general para la inclusión de las personas con discapacidad. Obtenido de https://www.sep.gob.mx/work/models/sep1/Resource/558c2c24-0b12-4676-ad90-8ab78086b184/ley_general_inclusion_personas_discapacidad.pdf

Discapacidad, C. N. (3 de Noviembre de 2016). Modelos educativos inclusivos.

Dussan, C. P. (2004). Derechos humanos y discapacidad. Colombia: Jurisprudencia.

Espejo, P. R. (Enero de 2009). Una maestra especial Maria Montesori. El chaparil, Nerja, Malaga.

Galvis, A. H. (1997). Ingeniería de Software Educativo. Ediciones Iniandes.

Hernández, G. (2001). Antropología de la discapacidad y dependencia. Madrid España.

Irazabal, A. L. (2011). Acuerdo 592 por el que se establece la articulación de la educación básica. Obtenido de http://www.sipi.siteal.iipe.unesco.org/sites/default/files/sipi_normativa/acuerdo_592_articulacion_educacion_basica_primaria.pdf

José Valdeni de Lima, F. S. (2014). Objetos de aprendizaje multimodales:proyectos y aplicaciones. Barcelona España: UOC.

Ley General para la inclusión de las personas con dicapacidad (Cámara de diputados del H. congreso de la unión, Secretaría de servicios parlamentarios 30 de Mayo de 2011).

María Celeste Gatto, V. G. (2005). Educación Especial en el niño srdo o con deficiencias auditivas. En M. S. Mina, Educando con capacidades diferentes (págs. 71-79). Córdoba Argentina: Brujas.

Mazariegos. (2006). Atención a niños con necesidades especiales.

Mina, M. S. (2005). Educando con capacidades diferentes (Vols. ISBN 987-591-008-2). Argentina: Bruja.

SEP. (30 de Diciembre de 2013). Programa Sectorial de educaciòn. Obtenido de https://www.sep.gob.mx/work/models/sep1/ Resource/4479/4/images/PROGRAMA_SECTORIAL_ DE_EDUCACION_2013_2018_WEB.pdf

SEP, S. d. (2002). Programa nacional de fortalecimiento de la educación especial y de la integración educativa. México.

Biographies of
The Coordinating Authors

José Víctor Galaviz Rodríguez, Ph.D. is a Full-Time, Tenured B-Level Research Professor, a Member of the National System of Technological and Scientific Evaluation RCEA-07-26884-2013 in Field 7, Engineering and Industry. He is a CONACYT grant recipient. He is also an Evaluator for the United Promep System (SISUP), He is a member of the Program for Professional Development in Higher Education. He is also a representative for the professors of the Academic Process Engineering department IES: UTTLAX-CA-2. He holds a Ph.D. in Strategic Planning and Technological Management, with an honorable mention for Research from UPAEP university (Puebla, Mexico).

Román Daniel Romero Mitre holds a Master's of Science degree in Engineering. He is a Full-Time C-Level Associate Research Professor. He is a member of the Industrial Maintenance faculty at Universidad Autónoma de Tlaxcala. He is a former CONACYT grant recipient for his Ph.D. studies at CIATEQ from 2016 to 2018. He is the coordinator of Dual Degree program in Industrial Operations and Process Engineering.

Alexis Christian Charbonnier Poeter is Head of Department, International Relations and Internship Coordinator and a Tenured Professor of English and Spanish in the Business Administration Department of the Institut Universitaire de Technologie of Université Clermont Auvergne in Aubière, France. He is a graduate of the Medill School of Journalism of Northwestern University, Evanston, Illinois, USA, and he completed all coursework for the Master's degree in Education at ITESM Instituto Tecnológico de Estudios Superiores de Monterrey, Mexico.

CPSIA information can be obtained
at www.ICGtesting.com
Printed in the USA
BVHW070837160919
558547BV00006B/48/P

9 781506 530017